LIVING ITALIAN

LIVING ITALIAN

MARIA VALGIMIGLI

Formerly Lecturer in Italian,
College of Commerce, Manchester

HODDER AND STOUGHTON
LONDON SYDNEY AUCKLAND TORONTO

Tape-recordings of *Living Italian* are available from Tutor-Tape Company Ltd, 2 Replingham Road, London SW18

ISBN 0 340 15629 5

First published 1960
Second edition: thirteenth impression 1978

Printed in Great Britain for Hodder and Stoughton Educational, a division of Hodder and Stoughton Ltd, Mill Road, Dunton Green, Sevenoaks, Kent
by Butler & Tanner Ltd, Frome and London

PREFACE

THIS Italian course is intended for students who are studying privately or attending Evening Classes. It is divided into three Sections, from Lessons I to X, XI to XX and XXI to XXX. At the end of each Section there are extra exercises in the form of a short test, which enable students to revise the work studied so far.

As it is important that students should acquire from the beginning an extensive vocabulary of everyday use, the Conversational Exercises at the end of each lesson should be carefully studied and put into practice. In all the Sections, it is recommended that Exercises A and B be done during the lesson, orally or in writing. Exercises C and D should be given as written homework and Exercise E as *preparation* for the following week. A short dictation of words or phrases from the lessons should be given by the teacher each week from the second lesson onwards, to enable the student to hear spoken Italian. From Lesson XI onwards, unseen dictations should be given, to prepare for the first examinations.

Once the student has mastered the first five lessons, Alphabet Games (*giochi dell'alfabeto*) such as the ones which appear at the end of Lessons VI and XII could serve as a revision of vocabulary.

In Sections II and III, in addition to the Grammar Rules, each lesson contains a list of words pertaining to Travel. Lessons XVII to XXIX take the student on a "Journey to Italy" and a little is mentioned about the places visited. With this extra vocabulary, students will have an opportunity to practise the conversation which is so essential in the study of a language.

It is hoped that when students have completed the course they will have acquired a love of the Italian language and will have been encouraged to continue with their study of Italy and her language.

M.V.

CONTENTS

SECTION ONE

SECTION TWO

SECTION THREE

INTRODUCTION

THE ALPHABET

The Italian alphabet consists of only 21 letters, which are as follows:

LETTER	PRONUNCIATION	LETTER	PRONUNCIATION
a	as *a* in car	n	ennay
b	bee	o	as *o* in not
c	chee	p	pee
d	dee	q	coo
e	ay	r	erray
f	effay	s	essay
g	dgee	t	tee
h	acca	u	oo
i	ee	v	voo
l	ellay	z	dzayta
m	emmay		

The letters **j** (i lunga), **k** (cappa), **w** (d*o*ppio voo), **x** (icks), **y** (*i*psilon), do not figure in the Italian alphabet; they are, however, used for the spelling of foreign words.[1]

y has been replaced by *i*:

e.g. gi*o*ia *joy* r*a*ion *rayon*

k is generally replaced by *ch*:

e.g. chilogramma *kilogramme*

The Greek combination *ph* has been replaced by *f*:

e.g. alfabeto *alphabet* fotografia *photograph, photography*

[1] *x* is also found in expressions such as *ex-presidente*, ex-president, *ex-cancelliere*, ex-chancellor, etc.

PRONUNCIATION

Vowels

a is pronounced *approximately* like *a* in *car*:
e.g. sala *room* caro *dear*

e has two sounds:
(1) like *e* in *bell* (known as the open *e*).
e.g. bello *beautiful* lento *slow*
(2) like *a* in *late* (known as the close *e*).
e.g. seta *silk* meno *less* pineta *pine grove*

i is pronounced like *i* in *marine*:
e.g. finire *to finish* primo *first*

o has two sounds:
(1) like *o* in *not* (known as the open *o*).
e.g. notte *night* opera *opera, work*
(2) like *o* in *note* (known as the close *o*).
e.g. nome *name* ora *hour*

u is always pronounced like *oo* in *moon*:
e.g. uno *one* musica *music*

Consonants

Of the sixteen consonants the following ten are pronounced approximately as in English: **b, d, f, l, m, n, p, q, t,** and **v.**

c has two sounds:
(1) like *c* in *can*, when followed by *a*, *o*, *u*, or by any consonant, including *h*.

e.g.	cane	*dog*	che	*what, that*
	con	*with*	chi	*who, whom*
	cura	*care, attention*	crudo	*raw*

(2) like *ch* in *chop*, when followed by *e* or *i*.
e.g. cena *supper* cima *top, summit*

cc before *e* or *i* is pronounced like *tch* in *match*:

e.g. faccia *face*

g has two sounds:

(1) like *g* in *go* when followed by *a*, *o*, *u*, or by any consonant, including *h*.

e.g. galante	*gallant*	grande	*big, great*
gola	*throat*	ghirlanda	*garland*
gufo	*owl*		

(2) like *g* in *ginger*, when followed by *e* or *i*.

e.g. gentile	*kind*	giardino	*garden*

gg before *e* or *i* is pronounced like *dg* in *edge*:

e.g. oggi *today*

h is always silent. Initial *h* is found only in:

ho	*I have*
hai	*you have* (familiar form)
ha	*he, she has*
hanno	*they have*

and in a few foreign words.

The letter *h* prevents confusion between these four forms of the verb *avere* (to have) and *o* (or), *ai* (to the), *a* (to, at), *anno* (year).

h is also found in a few exclamations:

e.g. ah! ahi! ahimè! *oh! ah! alas!*

q is always followed by *u* and has the same sound as *qu* in *quick*:

e.g. quanto	*how much*	qui	*here*
questo	*this*	quota	*share, quota*

r *or* **rr** is trilled in Italian:

e.g. carne	*meat*	carro	*cart*

s has two sounds:

(1) like *s* in *sad*, when beginning a word before any vowel.

e.g. sala	*hall*	sito	*site*
sette	*seven*	sole	*sun*

Also in compound words:
e.g. ventisei *twenty-six* trentasette *thirty-seven*
or when doubled:
e.g. basso *low* permesso *permission*
or before the consonants *c*, *f*, *p*, *q*, and *t*:
e.g. studio *study* squadra *team, group*
spuntino *snack, light refreshment*

(2) but when intervocalic it *usually* sounds like *s* in *rose*:
e.g. rosa *rose* vaso *vase*
and similarly when the noun ends in *ione*:
e.g. divisione *division* confusione *confusion*
and it is similarly pronounced before *b*, *d*, *g*, *l*, *m*, *n*, *r*, *v*.

z *or* **zz** also has two sounds:

(1) like *ts* in *bits*.
e.g. grazie *thanks, thank you* terrazza *terrace*

(2) like *ds* in *adds*.
e.g. pranzo *dinner* mezzo *half*

The following combined letters are of great importance:

ch like *ch* in chemist } can only be followed by *e* or *i*:
gh like *g* in *gun* }
e.g. cherubino *cherub* chiave *key*
Margherita *Margaret* laghi *lakes*

gli has a similar sound to *lli* in *million*:
e.g. luglio *July* Ventimiglia
except in a very few words where it has the same sound as in English:
e.g. Anglicano *Anglican* glicine *wistaria*
negligere *to neglect*

gn has a similar sound to *ni* in *union* or *gn* in *mignonette*:
e.g. ogni *each, every* signora *madam, lady*

gu before a vowel is always pronounced like *gw* in *Gwendoline*:
e.g. lingua *language, tongue* guida *guide*

sc before *e* or *i* is pronounced like *sh* in *ship*:

e.g.	scendere	*to go down, descend*
	uscire	*to go out*

but before *a*, *o*, *u*, and *h* it has a hard sound like *sk*:

e.g.	scala	*staircase*	scopo	*aim, purpose*
	scuro	*dark*	scherzo	*joke*

It will be noticed that the Italian language has no nasal sounds.

PUNCTUATION

Punctuation Marks

The punctuation marks are the same in Italian as in English:

.	punto	—	lineetta
,	virgola	“ ”	virgolette
;	punto e virgola	( )	parentesi
:	due punti	[ ]	parentesi quadra
?	punto interrogativo	*	asterisco
!	punto esclamativo	}	grappa
...	punti sospensivi		

They are used much in the same manner as in English, except in the following cases:

(1) The *punti sospensivi* are used in the place of the English dash.

(2) The *lineetta* denotes a change of speaker in a conversation.

The Apostrophe

The apostrophe is used when a letter has been elided:

e.g. l'amica *instead of* la amica.
l'Italia *instead of* la Italia.

Syllabication

Italian words are divided into syllables. The main rules are:

(1) Any single consonant between two vowels belongs to the syllable which follows.

e.g. matita (*pencil*) ma-ti-ta
parola (*word*) pa-ro-la

(2) All double consonants must be distinctly pronounced in Italian.

e.g. bello (*beautiful*) bel-lo
tetto (*roof*) tet-to

ACCENTUATION

Written accents

Three accents are used in Italian: the grave (`), the acute (´) and the circumflex (^).

(1) The grave accent is the one most frequently used. It acts mainly as a stress mark. This accent is used:

(*a*) to denote the open sound of *e*.

e.g. è	*is, it is*	caffè	*coffee*

(*b*) on words which have the stress on the last syllable.

e.g. città	*town, city*	virtù	*virtue*

(This category includes mainly words contracted from the Latin.)

(*c*) on the following five words.

ciò	*that*	più	*more*
già	*already*	può	*he* (*she*) *can*
giù	*down*		

(*d*) on words of one syllable which otherwise would be confused with others of the same spelling but of different meaning.

e.g.	è	*is*	e	*and*
	dà	*gives*	da	*by, from*
	dì	*day* (poet.)	di	*of*
	sì	*yes*	si	(pronoun) *himself, herself*
	là	*there*	la	(article) *the*
	sè	*himself, herself*	se	*if*
	lì	*there*	li	(pronoun) *them*
	tè	*tea*	te	*thee* (*you*)

(2) The acute accent is sometimes seen written in a word over the letter *e*, when the *e* has a close sound.

e.g. né *nor* perché *why, because*

This accent is frequently replaced by the grave accent.

(3) The circumflex accent is very rarely used. It is written only on words which have been contracted; such words are found only in poetry.

e.g. côrre *for* cogliere *to gather*

Stress or tonic accent

(1) In Italian the stress on words usually falls on the last syllable but one:

e.g. par*o*la *word* Mil*a*no *Milan*

In this case the words are known as *parole piane.*

(2) The stress is also found on the last syllable but two:

e.g. s*a*bato *Saturday* dom*e*nica *Sunday*
t*a*vola *table*

These are known as *parole sdrucciole.*

(3) Sometimes it is even found on the last syllable but three:

e.g. dim*e*nticano *they forget* des*i*derano *they want*

This is more uncommon and occurs chiefly in verbal forms; these are known as *parole bisdrucciole.*

(4) And, finally, there are words with the stress on the last syllable, but in this case the stress is indicated by a grave accent, as already stated above:

e.g. qualità *quality* carità *charity*

These are known as *parole tronche.*

Throughout this book, if the stress occurs other than as indicated in (1) *above, the stressed vowel is shown in italic type, or in roman type if the word itself is in italic.*

CAPITAL LETTERS

Capital letters are used in Italian as in English for names of people, countries, towns, rivers and lakes:

e.g. Roberto Italia Roma Como

But small letters are used as follows:

(1) For the months of the year, days of the week, seasons and adjectives of nationality.

e.g. aprile	*April*
lunedì	*Monday*
la primavera	*Spring*
la lingua italiana	*the Italian language*

(2) For titles followed by a proper name.

e.g. il signor Neri	*Mr. Neri*
la contessa Valli	*Countess Valli*

(3) For the pronoun I, *io*, unless it begins a sentence.

e.g. Io parlo italiano.	*I speak Italian.*
Anch'io.	*I, too.*

Note, however, that the pronouns *Lei* (singular form) and *Loro* (plural form), when meaning "you", are written with a capital letter:

e.g. Dove va Lei, signora?	*Where are you going, madam?*
Io vado a Milano.	*I am going to Milan.*
Anch'io.	*So am I.*

PRONUNCIATION PRACTICE

(1) Amica, regina, matita, caro, chiave, lago, laghi, grande, penna, ogni, f*i*glio, quasi, Roma, Milano, Bologna, Vinci, Rapallo, N*a*poli, Verona, G*e*nova, Firenze, Pisa, Torino, Ven*e*zia.

(2) Gr*a*zie. Prego. Permesso. Avanti. Presente. Assente. Buon giorno. Buona sera. Buona notte. Signore. Signora. Signorina.

(3) Uno, due, tre, quattro, cinque, sei, sette, otto, nove.

(4) Chi va piano va sano e va lontano.
Una r*o*ndine non fa primavera.
Il tempo fugge e non ritorna più.
Chi è paziente è sapiente.
La salute è la prima ricchezza.
A ogni uccello suo nido è bello.
Chi ben princ*i*pia è alla metà dell'*o*pera.
L'uomo propone e Dio dispone.
Bisogna b*a*ttere il ferro mentre è caldo.
*A*cqua cheta rovina i ponti.

SECTION ONE

LESSON 1

The Definite Article—*the*

The is translated by:

(*a*) *il* before a masculine noun in the singular beginning with a consonant, except *s* impure (that is, *s* followed by a consonant), *z* or *gn*.

e.g. il libro *the book* il ragazzo *the boy*

(*b*) *lo* before a masculine noun in the singular beginning with *s* impure, *z* or *gn*.

e.g. lo studente *the student* lo zio *the uncle*
lo gnocco *the dumpling*

(*c*) *la* before a feminine noun in the singular beginning with a consonant.

e.g. la penna	*the pen*
la studentessa	*the student*
la zia	*the aunt*

(*d*) *l'* before a masculine or a feminine noun in the singular beginning with a vowel.

e.g. l'alunno	*the pupil* (*m.*)
l'alunna	*the pupil* (*f.*)

Gender of Nouns

In Italian there are only two genders; every noun must be either masculine or feminine.

As a preliminary guide, it is useful to know that:

(*a*) Nouns ending in *-o* are masculine.

e.g. il libro	*the book*
il quaderno	*the exercise book*

There are only a few exceptions to this rule, the most common being:

la mano *the hand* la r*a*dio *the radio*

(*b*) Nearly all nouns ending in *-a* are feminine.

e.g. la penna	*the pen*	la matita	*the pencil*

For masculine nouns ending in *-a* (e.g. *il poeta*, poet), see Lesson XVI.

(*c*) Nouns ending in *-ione* are feminine.

e.g. la stazione	*the station*
la televisione	*the television*

(*d*) Nouns ending in *-e* may be of either gender. Those denoting people are easy to remember.

e.g. il padre	*the father*	la madre	*the mother*

Others may cause confusion.

e.g. la classe	*the classroom*	il nome	*the name*
l'animale (*m.*)	*the animal*	la frase	*the sentence*

Because of this, the student should try, from the beginning, to associate all nouns with their corresponding articles.

To form the feminine of nouns which denote people and which end in *-o*, change the *-o* to *-a*.

e.g. il maestro	*master*	→	la maestra	*mistress*
il ragazzo	*boy*	→	la ragazza	*girl*

VOCABULARY

la classe	class, classroom	la frase	phrase, sentence
il maestro	master, teacher	la r*a*dio	radio, wireless
la maestra	mistress	lo st*u*dio	study, studio
l'alunno	pupil (*m.*)	lo studente	student (*m.*)
l'alunna	pupil (*f.*)	la studentessa	student (*f.*)
la t*a*vola	table	lo zio	uncle
la s*e*dia	chair	la zia	aunt
la porta	door	il padre	father
il libro	book	la madre	mother
il quaderno	exercise book	e (*or* ed *before a vowel*)	and
la finestra	window		
il banco	desk	è	is (it is)
la penna	pen	chi ha?	who has?
la matita	pencil	dove?	where?
la stazione	station	dov'è?	where is?
la televisione	television	ecco	here is, here are, there is, there are
il nome	name		
l'animale (*m.*)	animal	sopra	on, upon

sotto	under	signore	sir
mi passi	pass me	signora	madam, Mrs.
mi mostri	show me	signorina	Miss
per favore / per piacere	please		

NOTE.—*Signore* (like all the other titles ending in *-ore*, as *senatore*, *professore*, *dottore*), drops the final *-e* before a name or title.

CONVERSATION

Buon giorno	*Good morning (day).*
Buona sera.	*Good evening.*
Come sta?	*How are you?*
Bene, grazie, e Lei?	*Well, thank you, and you?*
Molto bene, grazie.	*Very well, thank you.*

LA CLASSE

Ecco la classe. Ecco il maestro. Il libro è sopra la t*a*vola. Il quaderno è sopra il banco. Ecco l'alunno. L'alunno ha la matita. Ecco l'alunna. L'alunna ha la penna. Ecco la porta. Dov'è la finestra? Mi mostri la s*e*dia, per favore. Ecco la s*e*dia. Mi mostri la t*a*vola. Ecco la t*a*vola. Chi ha il libro? Il maestro ha il libro. Mi mostri il banco. Ecco il banco.

EXERCISES

A. Translate, and then answer in Italian, the following questions:

1. Dov'è il libro?
2. Dov'è la porta?
3. Chi ha il quaderno?
4. Chi ha la penna?
5. Dov'è la s*e*dia?
6. Dov'è il banco?
7. Chi ha la s*e*dia?
8. Chi ha la matita?
9. Dov'è l'alunno?
10. Dov'è l'alunna?

B. Put the correct form of the definite article in front of the following nouns:

1. — alunno
2. — maestro
3. — penna
4. — libro
5. — studente
6. — matita

7. — quaderno
8. — porta
9. — zio
10. — banco
11. — finestra
12. — zia

C. Translate into Italian:

1. The girl and the pencil.
2. The boy and the pen.
3. The master and the pupil (*m.*).
4. The mistress and the pupil (*f.*).
5. The door and the window.
6. The book and the exercise book.
7. Here is the student (*m.*).
8. Here is the student (*f.*).
9. Pass me the chair, please.
10. Thank you. Show me the table.

D. Translate into Italian:

1. Good morning, madam.
2. Good morning, sir.
3. How are you?
4. Well, thank you, and you?
5. Very well, thank you.
6. Where is the teacher (*f.*)?
7. Who has the book?
8. Show me the pencil, please.
9. Pass me the exercise book, please.
10. Thank you, madam.

E. Complete the following and then translate into English:

1. Il maestro ha — libro e — penna.
2. Mi mostri — televisione.
3. Dov'è — animale?
4. Per favore, signore, mi passi — s*e*dia.
5. Il quaderno è sotto — t*a*vola.
6. La matita è sopra — r*a*dio.
7. Mi mostri — quaderno, per favore.
8. Ecco — st*u*dio.
9. La ragazza ha — matita.
10. Dov'è — studente?

LESSON II

The Indefinite Article—*a, an*

A, *an* is translated by:

(*a*) *un* before masculine nouns in the singular, except those beginning with *s* impure or with *z*.

e.g. un libro *a book* un amico *a friend* (*m.*)

(*b*) *uno* before a masculine noun in the singular beginning with *s* impure, *z* or *gn*.

e.g. uno spillo *a pin* uno zio *an uncle*
uno gnomo *a gnome*

(*c*) *una* before a feminine noun in the singular beginning with a consonant.

e.g. una penna *a pen* una sala *a room*

(*d*) *un'* before a feminine noun in the singular beginning with a vowel.

e.g. un'amica *a friend* (*f.*) un'ora *an hour*

Cardinal Numbers

1	uno	5	cinque	9	nove
2	due	6	sei	10	dieci
3	tre	7	sette	11	*u*ndici
4	quattro	8	otto	12	d*o*dici

NOTE.—*uno*, with its different forms *un*, *una*, *un'* as explained above, is the only number which changes its form according to the noun which follows.

Formation of the Plural of Nouns

(*a*) Masculine nouns ending in *-o*, *-a* or *-e* change the final vowel to *-i*.

e.g. libro → libri padre → padri
poeta → poeti

(*b*) To form the plural of nouns ending in *-io* omit the *-o*, unless the *-i-* is stressed, in which case change *-io* to *-ii*.

e.g. fíglio → figli BUT zio → zii

(*c*) Feminine nouns ending in *-a* change *-a* to *-e*.

(*d*) Feminine nouns ending in *-e* change *-e* to *-i*.

e.g. madre → madri

NOTE.—The plural of the feminine noun *la mano* (hand) is *le mani*.

VOCABULARY

una casa	house	un'amica	friend (*f.*)
un giardino	garden	un'ora	hour
una sala	hall, room	uno spillo	pin
un salotto	lounge, living-room	che?	what?
		c'è	there is; is there?
una sala da pranzo	dining-room	chi è?	who is?
		che ha? *or* che cosa ha?	what has?
una cucina	kitchen		
un ragazzo	boy	questo, questa	this (*m.*), this (*f.*)
una ragazza	girl	a destra	to the right
un giornale	newspaper	a sinistra	to the left
una rivista	magazine	Maria	Mary
un amico	friend (*m.*)	Giovanni	John

CONVERSATION

Che (cosa) è questo?	*What is this?*
Permesso.	*Allow me; excuse me.*
Avanti.	*Forward, come in.*
Mi scusi.	*Excuse me.*
Prego.	*I beg you.*

UNA CASA

Ecco un giardino. Ecco una casa. Ecco una porta. A destra c'è la sala da pranzo. A sinistra c'è il salotto. Ecco la cucina. La casa ha quattro porte e sei finestre. Ecco il padre. Ecco la madre. Il padre ha un giornale. La madre

ha una rivista. Ecco una ragazza. Ecco due ragazze. Ecco un ragazzo. Ecco due ragazzi. Chi è questa ragazza? È Maria. Chi è questo ragazzo? È Giovanni. Maria ha un libro. Giovanni ha un quaderno.

EXERCISES

A. Translate, and then answer in Italian, the following questions:

1. Dov'è la casa?
2. Dov'è la porta?
3. Che c'è a sinistra?
4. Che c'è a destra?
5. Chi è questa ragazza?
6. Chi è questo ragazzo?
7. Che ha il padre?
8. Che ha la madre?
9. Che ha Maria?
10. Che ha Giovanni?

B. Put the correct form of the indefinite article in front of the following nouns:

1. — zia
2. — casa
3. — amico
4. — porta
5. — amica
6. — rivista
7. — ragazzo
8. — zio
9. — sala
10. — giornale
11. — padre
12. — studente

C. Translate into Italian:

1. A boy and a girl.
2. A father and a mother.
3. A student (*m.*) and a pupil (*f.*).
4. A house and a garden.
5. To the right there is a door.
6. To the left there is a window.
7. Here is a dining-room.
8. Here is a lounge.
9. A newspaper is on the chair.
10. A magazine is under the table.

D. Translate into Italian:

1. Good evening, sir.
2. Good evening, madam.
3. Where is the dining-room?
4. To the right, madam.
5. Where is the lounge?
6. To the left, sir.
7. What is this?
8. It is a magazine.
9. What is this?
10. It is a newspaper.

E. Complete with a noun:

1. Ecco un —
2. Ecco una —
3. Ecco un' —
4. Mi mostri una —
5. Chi ha uno —
6. Mi passi tre —
7. Mi mostri due —
8. Ecco cinque —
9. Ecco sette —
10. Ecco nove —

LESSON III

Plural of the Definite Article

The plural of *il*	is	*i*
The plural of *la*	is	*le*
The plural of *l'* (*m.*)	is	*gli*
The plural of *l'* (*f.*)	is	*le*
The plural of *lo*	is	*gli*

e.g.	il libro	→	i libri
	la penna	→	le penne
	l'alunno	→	gli alunni
	l'alunna	→	le alunne
	lo studente	→	gli studenti

NOTE.—*gli* generally becomes *gl'* before a word beginning with *i*: e.g. l'Italiano (*the Italian*) → gl'Italiani, but *gli Italiani* is also correct.

Agreement of Adjectives

All adjectives must agree in gender and number with the noun they qualify:

(*a*) If the adjective ends in *-o* the feminine is formed by changing the *-o* to *-a*.

e.g. nero (*black*) (*m.*) → nera (*f.*)
italiano (*Italian*) (*m.*) → italiana (*f.*)

The plural is formed by changing the *-o* to *-i* and the *-a* to *-e*.

e.g. un ragazzo italiano → due ragazzi italiani
una ragazza italiana → due ragazze italiane

(*b*) If the adjective ends in *-e*, it remains the same for the feminine singular. To form the plural for both genders change the *-e* to *-i*.

e.g. un ragazzo inglese → due ragazzi inglesi
una ragazza inglese → due ragazze inglesi

Position of Adjectives

The general rule for the position of adjectives is that they follow the noun, particularly where the adjective refers to colour, shape, nationality and religion.

e.g. un libro nero	*a black book*
una penna nera	*a black pen*
un libro quadrato	*a square book*
una t*a*vola rotonda	*a round table*
un signore italiano	*an Italian gentleman*
una signora italiana	*an Italian lady*
un signore anglicano	*an Anglican gentleman*
una signora catt*o*lica	*a Catholic lady*

Ordinal Numbers

1st	primo	5th	quinto
2nd	secondo	6th	sesto
3rd	terzo	7th	settimo
4th	quarto		

Ordinal numbers used as adjectives, agree with the noun they qualify and usually precede it.

e.g. il primo giorno	*the first day*
la prima settimana	*the first week*
i primi mesi	*the first months*
le prime lezioni	*the first lessons*

Days of the Week—*i giorni della settimana*

lunedì	*Monday*
martedì	*Tuesday*
mercoledì	*Wednesday*
giovedì	*Thursday*
venerdì	*Friday*
s*a*bato	*Saturday*
dom*e*nica	*Sunday*

As already stated, days of the week are written with a small initial letter (except, of course, when they begin a new sentence).

VOCABULARY

l'entrata	entrance
l'*a*lbero	tree
il fiore	flower
l'erba	grass
la f*o*glia	leaf
il gar*o*fano	carnation
il pap*a*vero	poppy
la rosa	rose
la margheritina	daisy
la farfalla	butterfly
il colore	colour
l'idea	idea
il mese	month
la lezione	lesson
bianco (-a)	white
nero (-a)	black
giallo (-a)	yellow
rosso (-a)	red
verde	green
celeste	pale blue
azzurro (-a)	blue
blu	blue
bruno (-a)	dark brown
marrone	brown
grande	big
p*i*ccolo (-a)	small
molto (-a)	much, a lot
molti (-e)	many
sì	yes
no	no
più	more
meno	less
di (*or* d' *before a vowel*)	of
ci sono	there are; are there?
dove sono?	where are?
quanto (-a)	how much (many)

CONVERSATION

Di che colore è questo?	*What colour is this?*
Che è questo?	*What is this?*
Che sono questi?	*What are these?*
Quanto fanno sette più tre?	*How many are seven plus three?* (lit. *How much make . . .?*)
Sei meno cinque fanno uno.	*Six minus five are one.*

UN GIARDINO

Ecco un giardino. Questo giardino è p*i*ccolo. Ecco un *a*lbero. Sotto l'*a*lbero c'è una p*i*ccola t*a*vola verde e ci sono due s*e*die verdi. Ci sono molti fiori in questo giardino, fiori rossi, gialli e celesti. Le f*o*glie di questi fiori sono verdi. L'erba è verde. Ecco un p*i*ccolo ragazzo. Il ragazzo ha tre fiori. Questi fiori sono pap*a*veri. Ecco una p*i*ccola ragazza. La ragazza ha dieci fiori, e questi fiori sono margheritine. La madre di questa ragazza ha quattro rose. Il padre ha due gar*o*fani. Ecco una farfalla; questa farfalla è gialla.

EXERCISES

A. Translate, and then answer in Italian, the following questions:

1. È grande il giardino?
2. Che c'è sotto l'*a*lbero?
3. Di che colore è l'erba?
4. Di che colore è la rosa?
5. Quanti pap*a*veri ha il ragazzo?
6. Quante margheritine ha la ragazza?
7. Chi ha quattro rose?
8. Chi ha due gar*o*fani?
9. Quanto fanno sei più due?
10. Quanto fanno nove meno quattro?

B. Translate into Italian:

1. Here is the garden.
2. Where is the entrance?
3. This table is round.
4. Where are the chairs?
5. There is a boy under the tree.
6. There are many butterflies in this garden.
7. What is this?
8. What are these?
9. Here is the teacher.
10. Here are the students.

C. Translate into English:

1. Questo signore è italiano.
2. Questa signora è inglese.
3. Questi ragazzi sono italiani.
4. Queste ragazze sono inglesi.
5. Ecco un quaderno rosso.
6. Ecco una matita gialla.
7. Ecco un libro verde.
8. Ecco due penne nere.
9. Dieci più due fanno d*o*dici.
10. *U*ndici meno due fanno nove.

D. Translate into Italian:

1. One red rose and two carnations.
2. One butterfly and three flowers.
3. Four tables.
4. Five gardens.
5. Six trees.
6. Seven flowers.
7. This red book.
8. This black pen.
9. These yellow flowers.
10. These green pencils.

E. Put the correct plural form of the definite article in front of the following nouns:

1. — fiori
2. — rose
3. — colori
4. — idee
5. — giorni
6. — studenti
7. — gar*o*fani
8. — zie
9. — case
10. — giardini

LESSON IV

Subject Pronouns

The personal subject pronouns are:

io	*I*
tu	*you (familiar form sing.)*
egli, lui, esso	*he, it*
ella, lei, essa	*she, it*
Lei	*you (polite form masc. and fem. sing.)*
noi	*we*
voi	*you (familiar form pl.)*
essi, loro	*they (masc.)*
esse, loro	*they (fem.)*
Loro	*you (polite form masc. and fem. pl.)*

In Italian the subject pronouns are often omitted before the verb as nearly all the verbal forms may be recognized by their terminations. These pronouns must, however, be used in the following cases:

(a) For emphasis.

e.g. Io non parlo italiano, signora.
I do not speak Italian, madam.

(*b*) When there are two subjects in contrast.

e.g. Carlo parla italiano, io parlo francese.
Charles speaks Italian, I speak French.

(*c*) After the word *anche* (too, also, even).

e.g. Roberto parla francese, anch'io parlo francese.
Robert speaks French, I too speak French.

egli (fem. *ella*) and *lui* (fem. *lei*) are used only for persons.

egli and *ella* are used in writing, *lui* and *lei* in conversation, and for emphasis.

esso (fem. *essa*) is used for persons, animals or things.

NOTE.—*it*, used as a subject pronoun, is seldom expressed in Italian.

e.g. Dov'è il giornale? È sopra la tavola.
Where is the newspaper? It is on the table.
Dov'è? *Where is it?*

The translation of "you"

In Italian there are four ways of translating *you* as a subject pronoun, viz: *tu*, *Lei*, *voi* and *Loro*.

(*a*) *tu*, known as the "familiar" form, is used when speaking (or writing) to a relation, an intimate friend, a child or an animal. The plural of *tu* is *voi*.

e.g. Tu parli italiano molto bene, Roberto.
You speak Italian very well, Robert.
Voi pronunziate bene queste parole, ragazzi.
You pronounce these words well, children.

(*b*) *Lei*, known as the "polite" form, is used when addressing a lady or a gentleman with whom one is not on intimate terms. The plural of *Lei* is *Loro*. This form is derived from an old expression similar to *Your Lordship* or *Your Ladyship*. *Lei* must be followed by the verb in the third person singular, *Loro* by the verb in the third person plural. *Lei* and *Loro* are spelt with a capital letter.

e.g. Lei è molto gentile, signora.
You are very kind, madam.
Loro sono molto gentili, signori.
You are very kind, gentlemen.
Come sta, signora? *How are you, madam?*
(*Lei* being understood).
Come stanno, signorine? *How are you, ladies?*
(*Loro* being understood).

(*c*) *voi*, besides being the plural form of *tu*, is used in commerce, and in some parts of Italy for addressing an individual.

e.g. Il prezzo che voi domandate è alto.
The price you are asking is high.
Che fate voi, ragazzo?
What are you doing, boy?

The Auxiliary Verbs *avere* and *essere*

Now let us study the present indicative of the auxiliary verbs *avere* (to have) and *essere* (to be) with all the subject pronouns.

PRESENT INDICATIVE

AVERE, *to have*		ESSERE, *to be*	
io ho	*I have*	io sono	*I am*
tu hai	*you have*	tu sei	*you are*
egli, lui, esso } ha	*he, it has*	egli, lui, esso } è	*he, it is*
ella, lei, essa } ha	*she, it has*	ella, lei, essa } è	*she, it is*
Lei } ha	*you have*	Lei } è	*you are*
noi abbiamo	*we have*	noi siamo	*we are*
voi avete	*you have*	voi siete	*you are*
essi, loro } hanno	*they have*	essi, loro } sono	*they are*
esse, loro } hanno	*they have*	esse, loro } sono	*they are*
Loro } hanno	*you have*	Loro } sono	*you are*

NOTE.—To form the negative, place *non* in front of the verb:

e.g. io non ho *I have not* io non sono *I am not*

To form the interrogative simply invert the pronoun and the verb:

e.g. ho io? *Have I?* sono io? *Am I?*

Very often the Italians form the interrogative by leaving the verb and pronoun as they stand and **either** by inflecting the voice, as one sometimes does in English when denoting surprise:

e.g. Lei ha una macchina? *You have a car?*
Giovanni ha un telefono? *Has John got a telephone?*

or by using *non è vero?* (is it not?):

e.g. Il libro è caro, non è vero? *The book is dear, is it not?*
La tavola è rotonda, non è vero? *The table is round, isn't it?*

(*Non è vero* is equivalent to the French *n'est-ce pas*.)

Months of the Year—*i mesi dell'anno*

gennaio	*January*	luglio	*July*
febbraio	*February*	agosto	*August*
marzo	*March*	settembre	*September*
aprile	*April*	ottobre	*October*
maggio	*May*	novembre	*November*
giugno	*June*	dicembre	*December*

VOCABULARY

il pranzo	dinner	l'ora	hour, the time
la credenza	sideboard	il figlio	son
la tovaglia	tablecloth	la figlia	daughter
il tovagliolo	serviette, table napkin	i figli	the children (sons and daughters)
il vaso	vase		
il piatto	plate, dish	pronto	ready
il coltello	knife	il signor Valli	Mr. Valli
la forchetta	fork	Mario	Mario
il cucchiaio	spoon	Pietro	Peter
il bicchiere	glass	quale *or* qual	which

UNA SALA DA PRANZO

Ecco una sala da pranzo. In questa sala c'è una grande tavola, ci sono sei sedie ed una credenza a sinistra. Sopra la tavola c'è una tovaglia bianca, e c'è un vaso di fiori; questi fiori sono rose. Ci sono piatti, coltelli, forchette, cucchiai, bicchieri e tovaglioli. Il pranzo è pronto. Ecco il padre, il signor Valli, la madre, la signora Valli, e i due figli, Pietro e Mario.

EXERCISES

A. Translate, then answer in Italian:

1. Che c'è in questa sala da pranzo?
2. E che c'è sopra la tavola?
3. Quante sedie ci sono?

4. Che c'è a sinistra?
5. Che fiori sono in questo vaso?
6. Chi è il padre?
7. Chi è la madre?
8. Chi sono i due figli?
9. Qual è il primo mese dell'anno?
10. Qual è il secondo mese?

B. Put the subject pronoun before these verbal forms:

1. — abbiamo
2. — è
3. — ho
4. — siamo
5. — hai
6. — siete
7. — sei
8. — sono
9. — ha
10. — hanno

C. Put a suitable adjective after the following nouns:

1. Il padre è —
2. La madre è —
3. Ecco un fiore —
4. Ecco una t*a*vola —
5. Questa sala da pranzo è —
6. Questo vaso è —
7. Questi fiori sono —
8. Queste s*e*die sono —
9. I pap*a*veri sono —
10. L'erba è —

D. Translate into Italian:

1. I have
2. He has
3. We have
4. She is
5. We are
6. You (polite form sing.) are
7. They have
8. I am
9. You (polite form pl.) have
10. We are not

E. Translate:

1. Three knives
2. Four forks
3. Two glasses
4. Five hours
5. The second month
6. The fourth day
7. The first year
8. We have a small house.
9. You (sing.) are Italian.
10. I haven't a glass.

LESSON V

Interrogatives

Chi *who, whom?*
Che, Che cosa, Cosa — *what?*

(Chi, Che, Che cosa, Cosa) are pronouns and they are invariable.

e.g. Chi è questo ragazzo?	*Who is this boy?*
Chi è questa ragazza?	*Who is this girl?*
Chi sono queste signore?	*Who are these ladies?*

The words *dove*, where? (usually *dov'* before a vowel), *come*, how? and *perchè*, why? are also invariable.

e.g. Dov'è Maria?	*Where is Mary?*
Dov'è Giovanni?	*Where is John?*
Dove sono le signore?	*Where are the ladies?*
Come sta?	*How are you?*
Perchè non compra Lei una villa?	*Why do you not buy a villa?*

NOTE.—*perchè* also means *because*:

Perchè io non ho danaro. *Because I have no money.*

The following interrogatives may be used as pronouns or adjectives, but they are variable and therefore agree in number and gender with their nouns.

Quanto?	*How much?*	Quale?	*Which?*
Quanti?	*How many?*	Qual?	*Which?*

Used adjectivally:	Quanto danaro?	*How much money?*
	Quanta carne?	*How much meat?*
	Quanti giorni?	*How many days?*
	Quante settimane?	*How many weeks?*
	Qual giorno?	*Which day?*
	Quali settimane?	*Which weeks?*
Used as pronouns:	Quale?	*Which one?*
	Quali?	*Which ones?*
	Quanti?	*How many?*

e.g. Ho due penne, quale preferisce?
I have two pens, which one do you prefer?
Ecco dei giornali inglesi, quali des*i*dera?
Here are some English newspapers, which ones do you want?

Plurals of Nouns ending in *-co, -go, -ca, -ga*

Nouns and adjectives ending in *-co* and *-go* generally insert *h* in the plural to keep the hard sound. The general rule is:

If the stress falls on the last syllable but one, insert the *h*, otherwise change the *-o* to *-i* in the normal way:

e.g.	il fuoco	*fire*	→	i fuochi
	lungo	*long*	→	lunghi
	tedesco	*German*	→	tedeschi
BUT	il m*e*dico	*doctor*	→	i m*e*dici
	magn*i*fico	*magnificent*	→	magn*i*fici

There are exceptions, however, two of which are:

l'amico	*friend*	→	gli amici
greco	*Greek*	→	greci

Feminine nouns and adjectives ending in *-ca* and *-ga* always take *h* in the plural:

e.g.	la barca	*boat*	→	le barche
	lunga	*long*	→	lunghe
	magn*i*fica	*magnificent*	→	magn*i*fiche

Conjugation of Regular Verbs

Italian verbs are divided into three conjugations; these are determined by their infinitive endings.

The First Conjugation ends in *-are*.
The Second Conjugation ends in *-ere*.
The Third Conjugation ends in *-ire*.

e.g.	parlare	*to speak*
	vendere	*to sell*
	capire	*to understand*

The stem or root of all regular verbs never changes (the stem is the part preceding the infinitive ending:

e.g. parl-are vend-ere cap-ire)

Different endings are added to the stem to denote the person, the number, the tense and the mood.

With *parlare* and *vendere* as model verbs of the first and second conjugations, now let us study the present indicative, together with the subject pronouns. The third conjugation will be studied in Lesson VI.

Present Indicative

PARLARE, *to speak*		VENDERE, *to sell*	
io parlo	*I speak*	io vendo	*I sell*
tu parli	*you speak*	tu vendi	*you sell*
egli } parla	*he speaks*	egli } vende	*he sells*
ella } parla	*she speaks*	ella } vende	*she sells*
Lei } parla	*you speak*	Lei } vende	*you sell*
noi parliamo	*we speak*	noi vendiamo	*we sell*
voi parlate	*you speak*	voi vendete	*you sell*
essi } parlano	*they (m.) speak*	essi } vendono	*they (m.) sell*
esse } parlano	*they (f.) speak*	esse } vendono	*they (f.) sell*
Loro } parlano	*you speak*	Loro } vendono	*you sell*

The Italian present translates not only the simple present "I speak", but also the progressive "I am speaking" and the emphatic "I do speak".

NOTE.—The verb "to do" used as an auxiliary is *not* translated in Italian.

Note the following common endings in the present indicative of all regular verbs:

The first person singular ends in *-o*.
The second person singular ends in *-i*.
The third person singular ends in *-a* or *-e*.
The first person plural ends in *-iamo*.
The second person plural ends in *-ate -ete -ite* (Lesson VI)
The third person plural ends in *-ano* or *-ono*.

Verbs conjugated like *parlare*: and like *vendere*:

comprare	*to buy*	ricevere	*to receive*
entrare	*to enter* (followed by the preposition *in* before nouns)	credere	*to believe*
domandare	*to ask*	ripetere	*to repeat*
mostrare	*to show*	perdere	*to lose*
trovare	*to find*		

NOTE.—The infinitive of the above verbs in *-ere* has the stress on the third syllable from the end, like e*ssere*.

As already stated, the subject pronouns are rarely used in Italian, except for clarity or emphasis.

In conversation, *lui* (he) and *lei* (she) with the plural *loro* (they) are used in preference to the other third person pronouns. (Note the small initial letter, and do not confuse these pronouns with *Lei* and *Loro*, the polite forms for "you".)

VOCABULARY

la città (*pl.* città)	town	parlare	to speak
in città	in town, into town	vendere	to sell
l'edif*i*cio	building	le quattro stagioni	the four seasons
la cattedrale / il duomo	cathedral	la primavera	spring
la chiesa	church	l'estate (*f.*)	summer
il munic*i*pio	town hall	l'autunno	autumn
il museo	museum	l'inverno	winter
la piazza	square	lungo	long
il viale	avenue	largo	wide
la via	road, street	corto	short
la sc*a*tola	box	stretto	narrow
il fazzoletto	handkerchief	l'anno	year
la stagione	season	dell'anno	of the year
tutto (-a)	all	il danaro (*or* denaro)	money
alcuno, alcuni / alcuna, alcune	some, any	il neg*o*zio	shop
altro	other	l'*u*ltimo	last
		con	with

IN CITTÀ

In una città ci sono molti edifici. In questa piazza, a sinistra c'è una cattedrale, a destra c'è un museo. In un'altra piazza c'è il muni*ci*pio. Alcune vie sono lunghe, altre sono corte. I viali sono lunghi e larghi. Due signore *e*ntrano in un neg*o*zio e c*o*mprano una tov*a*glia bianca e d*o*dici tovaglioli. Una signorina compra una sc*a*tola con sei fazzoletti. Le quattro stagioni dell'anno sono la primavera, l'estate, l'autunno, l'inverno. La primavera è la prima stagione, l'inverno è l'*u*ltima.

EXERCISES

A. Translate, then answer in Italian:

1. Che c'è in questa piazza, a destra?
2. E che c'è a sinistra?
3. Dov'è il muni*ci*pio?
4. Sono larghe tutte le vie?
5. Sono stretti i viali?
6. Dove *e*ntrano le due signore?
7. Che c*o*mprano?
8. Che compra la signorina?
9. Quanti giorni ci sono in una settimana?
10. Quante stagioni ci sono in un anno?

B. Put a suitable subject pronoun in front of the following verbs and translate:

1. — compriamo
2. — parlo
3. — vende
4. — trovate
5. — non riceve
6. — credo
7. — non compra
8. — v*e*ndono
9. — mostri
10. — riceviamo

C. Translate into Italian:

1. I do not sell
2. We buy
3. She believes
4. I am speaking
5. They believe
6. We find
7. He speaks
8. I lose
9. They find
10. You (*tu, voi, Lei, Loro*) buy

D. Put into the plural:

1. Questo fazzoletto è bianco.
2. Questa sc*a*tola è bianca.
3. Il giardino è lungo.
4. La porta è larga.
5. Questo ragazzo è tedesco.
6. Questa ragazza è tedesca.
7. Questo signore compra la casa.
8. Questa signora parla italiano.
9. L'alunno passa il quaderno.
10. L'alunna ripete la lezione.

E. Translate into English:

1. A destra c'è il munic*i*pio.
2. A sinistra c'è un neg*o*zio.
3. Ci sono due chiese in questa via.
4. Mi passi la rivista francese, per favore.
5. Dov'è il museo, signora, per favore?
6. Mi scusi, signore, dov'è il duomo?
7. Che è questo?
8. È un giornale tedesco.
9. Che sono questi?
10. Sono due giornali tedeschi.

LESSON VI

Regular Verbs (*continued*)

In the third conjugation the verbs are in two groups:

(1) those conjugated like *capire*, to understand.

(2) those conjugated like *servire*, to serve.

The endings of the present indicative are the same for both groups, but those in the first group take *-isc-* between the stem and the ending in all the persons of the singular and in the third person plural.

Now let us study a model verb in each of the groups. (See page 173 for further examples.)

Present Indicative

CAPIRE, *to understand*

io capisco	*I understand* or *I do understand*
tu capisci	*you understand*
egli	*he understands*
ella } capisce	*she understands*
Lei	*you understand*
noi capiamo	*we understand*
voi capite	*you understand*
essi	*they (m.) understand*
esse } capiscono	*they (f.) understand*
Loro	*you understand*

SERVIRE, *to serve*

io servo	noi serviamo
tu servi	voi servite
egli	essi
ella } serve	esse } servono
Lei	Loro

The *negative* is, as already stated, formed by placing *non* before the verb:

e.g. io non capisco	*I do not understand*
io non servo	*I do not serve*

The *interrogative* is formed **either** by placing the subject after the verb:

e.g. capisce Lei?	*do you understand?*
cap*i*scono i ragazzi?	*do the boys understand?*

or by mere intonation of the voice.

Prepositions

a	*to, at*	su	*on*
da	*from, by*	per	*for*
di	*of*	con	*with*
in	*in*		

These prepositions are used in the normal way before the indefinite article:

e.g. a un ragazzo	*to a boy*
da una signora	*from a lady*

NOTE.—Do not elide *da*.

Contractions of Prepositions

However, when these prepositions precede the definite article, they are joined to it and form one word:

e.g. al ragazzo (a + il)	*to the boy*
dalla signora (da + la)	*from the lady*

Now let us take the preposition *a* with all the different forms of the definite article.

a + il	→ al	e.g. al ragazzo
a + la	→ alla	alla ragazza
a + l'	→ all'	all'alunno
		all'alunna
a + lo	→ allo	allo studente
		allo zio

a + i → ai ai ragazzi
a + gli → agli agli studenti
agli zii
agli alunni

NOTE ALSO.—

from the, da + il → dal
da + la → dalla, *etc.*

of the, di + il → del
di + la → della, *etc.*

in the, in + il → nel
in + la → nella, *etc.*

on the, su + il → sul
su + la → sulla, *etc.*

The prepositions *con* (with) and *per* (for) usually contract only with the masculine *il* and *i*, or they may be written as two words if desired—both ways are correct:

e.g. col (*or* con il) ragazzo pel (*or* per il) ragazzo
coi (*or* con i) ragazzi pei (*or* per i) ragazzi

All the other contractions with *con* and *per* are now obsolete, and the use of both *pel* and *pei* is tending to die out.

This table will help the student to see, at a glance, the prepositions contracted with the definite article:

	+ il	+ la	+ l'	+ lo	+ i	+ le	+ gli
a (*to, at*)	al	alla	all'	allo	ai	alle	agli
da (*from, by*)	dal	dalla	dall'	dallo	dai	dalle	dagli
di (*of*)	del	della	dell'	dello	dei	delle	degli
in (*in*)	nel	nella	nell'	nello	nei	nelle	negli
su (*on*)	sul	sulla	sull'	sullo	sui	sulle	sugli
per (*for*)	pel *or* per il	per la	per l'	per lo	pei *or* per i	per le	per gli
con (*with*)	col *or* con il	con la	con l'	con lo	coi *or* con i	con le	con gli

Possession

In Italian, possession is shown by the use of the preposition *di* (usually *d'* before a vowel). There is no equivalent to the English apostrophe *s*.

e.g. il libro di Maria	*Mary's book*
la penna d'Anna	*Ann's pen*
il libro del ragazzo	*The boy's book*
le penne dei ragazzi	*The children's pens*

VOCABULARY

la campagna	country	pieno	full
in campagna	in *or* into the country	altrettanto a Lei	the same to you
il sole	sun	dentro	inside
l'uccello	bird	fuori	outside
la giornata	whole day	ora, adesso	now
il cestino	basket	spl*e*ndere	to shine
la cosa	thing	cantare	to sing
il pane	bread	passare	to pass, spend (*time*)
il form*a*ggio	cheese	aprire	to open
il prosciutto	ham	tirare	to draw, pull
la bott*i*glia	bottle	tirare fuori	to pull out
la limonata	lemonade	cominciare	to begin
l'aranciata	orangeade	mangiare	to eat
la frutta (*pl.* le frutta)	fruit	vedere	to see
la colazione	lunch	dice (*from* dire, *to say*)	(he) says
Roberto	Robert	risp*o*ndere	to reply
Anna	Ann	la domanda	question
vicino a	near	l'*a*cqua	water
lontano da	far from		

NOTE.—*vicino* (near) is followed by *a*:

e.g. vicino a Lei — *near you*

entrare (to enter) is followed by the preposition *in* before a noun:

e.g. entriamo in una casa — *we enter a house*

cominciare (to begin) is followed by the preposition *a* before another verb:

e.g. cominciamo a parlare — *we begin to speak*

IN CAMPAGNA

È primavera, il sole splende e gli uccelli *ca*ntano. Roberto e tre altri ragazzi p*a*ssano la giornata in campagna. Ora sono sotto un *a*lbero e vicino all'*a*lbero hanno un cestino. Che c'è in questo cestino? Molte cose per la colazione dei ragazzi. Roberto apre il cestino e tira fuori pane, form*a*ggio, prosciutto, frutta e due bott*i*glie. Una bott*i*glia è piena di limonata, l'altra è piena d'aranciata. È l'ora di colazione—i ragazzi com*i*nciano a mangiare. Una signora vede i ragazzi e dice (*says*)—Buon appetito.—Grazie, altrettanto a Lei, signora, risp*o*ndono i ragazzi.

EXERCISES

A. Answer in Italian:

1. Dove sono Roberto e gli altri tre ragazzi?
2. Che c'è vicino all'*a*lbero?
3. Che c'è nel cestino?
4. Chi apre il cestino?
5. Che c'è in una bott*i*glia?
6. E nell'altra?
7. Che dice la signora?
8. Che risp*o*ndono i ragazzi?
9. Capisce Lei questa lezione?
10. Chi risponde alle domande?

B. Translate into English:

1. Della signora
2. Sul libro
3. Dall'alunno
4. Nello st*u*dio
5. Al maestro
6. Con gli studenti
7. Pel signore
8. Con la zia
9. Nel giardino
10. Dagli zii

C. Translate:

1. I ragazzi cap*i*scono quasi (*almost*) tutto.
2. Noi rispondiamo alle domande.
3. Il maestro non è nello st*u*dio.
4. I giornali sono sulla t*a*vola.
5. La frutta è nel cestino.
6. Questa bott*i*glia è piena d'acqua.
7. Sotto questa s*e*dia c'è una rivista.
8. Ecco i libri della ragazza.
9. Questo uccello canta bene.
10. I quaderni degli studenti sono sull'erba.

D. Translate into Italian:

1. There is a bottle on the grass.
2. There are two boys near the tree.
3. The sun is not shining now.
4. A bird is singing.
5. I do not see the bird.
6. We begin to speak Italian.
7. I do not understand.
8. Do you understand, Robert?
9. The students reply well.
10. Here is a book for you, Madam.

E. Translate:

(*a*) 1. The lady's basket
2. The boy's hand
3. Anna's lunch
4. Two bottles of lemonade
5. Near the house
6. Far from the tree
7. In the basket
8. Of the girl
9. To the gentleman
10. From the master

(*b*) Write the present indicative of *avere* and *e*ssere** in the negative form, e.g. io non ho, *etc.*, io non sono, *etc.*

Il Primo Gioco dell'Alfabeto

This "Alphabet Game" is intended to help the student to revise the vocabulary studied in the lessons; the Italian translations of the given words will be found to be in alphabetical order.

e.g. 1.	August	agosto
2.	(the) glass	(il) bicchiere
3.	(the) house	(la) casa, *etc.*

NOTE.—The article must not be omitted, but should be placed, in brackets, before or after the noun, as the student wishes.

Now translate into Italian:

1.		April	a......
2.		white	b......
3.	(the)	knife	c......
4.		Sunday	d......
5.		here is, here are	e......
6.		February	f......
7.	(the)	garden	g......
8.		have you? (polite form)	h......
9.	(the)	winter	i......
10.		July	l......
11.	(the)	pencil	m......
12.		nine	n......
13.		October	o......
14.	(the)	first	p......
15.		this	q......
16.	(the)	rose	r......
17.	(the)	student	s......
18.	(the)	table	t......
19.		eleven	u......
20.		Friday	v......
21.	(the)	uncle	z......

LESSON VII

Direct Object Pronouns

The direct object pronouns are:

mi	*me*
ti	*you*
lo	*him* or *it* (*m.*)
la	*her* or *it* (*f.*)
La	*you* (*m.* or *f. sing., polite form*)
ci	*us*
vi	*you*
li	*them* (*m.*)
le	*them* (*f.*)
Li	*you* (*m. pl., polite form*)
Le	*you* (*f. pl., polite form*)

They are placed immediately before the verb except in a few cases which will be explained later.

e.g.	*I see him* or *it*	io *lo* vedo
	I see her or *it*	io *la* vedo
	We see them (*m.*)	noi *li* vediamo
	We see them (*f.*)	noi *le* vediamo
	Mary sees me	Maria *mi* vede
	I have it	io *l'*ho
	We invite him	noi *l'*invitiamo
	You invite us	Lei *c'*invita

NOTE.—*mi*, *ti*, *lo*, *la* and *vi* drop the vowel and take an apostrophe before a verb beginning with a vowel or *h*; but *ci* becomes *c'* only before *e* or *i*, as otherwise the *c* would become hard.

The Partitive Construction—*some, any*

(*a*) "Some" or "any" before a noun is usually translated by *di* and the contracted form of the definite article, when it stands for a part of something:

e.g. del pane — *some bread*
della carne — *some meat*
degli spinaci — *some spinach*
dell'acqua — *some water*
Ha (Lei) del pane? — *Have you any bread?*

However, it is omitted in negative sentences if the noun is collective or plural:

e.g. Non ho pane. *I have no bread* or *I haven't any bread.*
Non abbiamo libri. *We have no books.*

It may also be omitted in cases of enumeration:

e.g. Ho penne, matite e libri. *I have pens, pencils and books.*

(*b*) "Some" or "any" is translated by *alcuno*, with its different forms *alcuna* (*f.*) *alcuni* (*m. pl.*) and *alcune* (*f. pl.*), by *qualche*, when "some" or "any" indicates "a few", or by *un poco* (*un po'*), "a little":

e.g. un po' di pane — *a little bread*

Alcuno (rarely used in the singular) agrees in gender and number with the noun to which it refers:

e.g. alcuni libri — *some books*
alcune penne — *some pens*

Qualche must be followed by a noun in the singular, and any adjective or verb used in connection with it must also be in the singular:

e.g. qualche libro — *some books*
Qualche libro italiano è sulla sedia.
Some Italian books are on the chair.

VOCABULARY

il mare	sea	il tempo	weather, time
al mare	at the seaside	il bagno	bathe, bath
la vacanza	holiday	il costume da bagno	bathing costume
la fam*i*glia	family	l'asciugamano	towel
l'*a*ria	air	l'ombrellone	large umbrella
il sole	sun	la s*e*dia a sdr*a*io	deckchair
la salute	health		

il vino	wine	abbronzato	bronzed, tanned
il pane	bread	sano	healthy
la carne	meat	calmo	calm
lo z*u*cchero	sugar	agitato	rough (sea)
la cabina	cabin	mare grosso	rough sea
la spi*a*ggia	beach	forte	strong
la fine	end	quasi	almost
sempre	always	molto tempo	long time
spesso	often	un poco *or* un po'	a little
durante	during	affittare	to rent, hire
una volta	once	portare	to carry, bring
due volte	twice	imparare	to learn
qualche volta	sometimes	dopo	after
ma	but		

AL MARE

Durante i mesi d'estate, giugno, l*u*glio ed agosto, molte fam*i*glie p*a*ssano le vacanze al mare. L'*a*ria del mare è sana. Sulla spi*a*ggia ci sono cabine con t*a*vole e s*e*die. Alcune fam*i*glie aff*i*ttano una cabina per due o tre settimane; p*o*rtano i costumi da bagno e gli asciugamani e p*a*ssano molte ore sulla spi*a*ggia. Il mare non è sempre calmo, qualche volta è agitato. Il sole è forte durante i mesi di l*u*glio e d'agosto ma ci sono gli ombrelloni e, sotto questi ombrelloni, le s*e*die a sdr*a*io. I ragazzi p*a*ssano molto tempo nel mare e, dopo un bagno, hanno sempre buon appetito. Alla fine delle vacanze sono abbronzati dal sole.

EXERCISES

A. Answer in Italian:

1. Quali sono i mesi d'estate?
2. Dove passa (Lei) le vacanze d'estate?
3. È sempre calmo il mare?
4. Che c'è sulla spi*a*ggia?
5. Che c'è sotto gli ombrelloni?
6. È sana l'*a*ria del mare?
7. Che preferisce Lei, il mare o la campagna?
8. Dove p*a*ssano molto tempo i ragazzi?
9. È lontano da questa città il mare?
10. È vicina la campagna?

B. Complete with the partitive article and translate:

1. Maria ha — penne.
2. Roberto ha — libri.
3. Ecco — studenti.
4. Ecco — studentesse.
5. Io ho — acqua fresca.
6. Lei ha — vino rosso.
7. Questa signora compra — riviste.
8. Questo signore compra — giornali.
9. Ha Lei — zii?
10. Hanno Loro — amiche?

C. Translate:

1. Mary understands it (*f*).
2. John learns it (*m*.).
3. We find them (*m*.).
4. They lose them (*f*.).
5. We see you (*familiar form*).
6. Anna sees us.
7. We have them (*f*.).
8. I have them (*m*.).
9. Anna has it (*f*.).
10. They do not have it (*m*.).

D. Complete with a noun:

1. Io ho del —
2. Noi abbiamo della —
3. Essi c*o*mprano dello —
4. Il maestro mostra dei —
5. Maria compra delle —
6. Non capisco la —
7. Anna compra un —
8. La signora vede il —
9. Il signore vede la —
10. Noi affittiamo una —

E. Translate:

1. We do not see the beach.
2. You find a cabin.

3. They speak to the lady.
4. He understands this lesson.
5. She buys some bread.
6. I buy some sugar.
7. Have you any Italian friends (*m.*)?
8. No, I have no Italian friends (*m.*).
9. Have they any English friends (*f.*)?
10. Yes, they have many English friends (*f.*).

F. Write the present tense of *comprare* and *vendere* in the negative form.

1. non compro, *etc.* 2. non vendo, *etc.*

LESSON VIII

Indirect Object Pronouns

The indirect object pronouns are:

mi	*to me*	ci	*to us*
ti	*to you*	vi	*to you*
gli	*to him*	loro	*to them* (*m.* and *f.*)
le	*to her*		
Le	*to you* (*m.* and *f.*)	Loro	*to you* (*m.* and *f.*)

These pronouns, with the exception of *loro* and *Loro*, usually precede the verb, except in certain cases which will be explained in a later lesson.

e.g. Maria *mi* parla.	*Mary is speaking to me.*
Io *le* parlo.	*I am speaking to her.*
Roberto *ci* parla.	*Robert is speaking to us.*
Noi *gli* parliamo.	*We are speaking to him.*
Giovanni parla *Loro*.	*John is speaking to you* (*pl.*).
Noi parliamo *loro*.	*We are speaking to them.*
Io *gli* mando una lettera.	*I send him a letter.*

Note.—The object is indirect when it is preceded by *to* or when *to* is understood, as in the last example.

Cardinal Numbers (*continued*)

13	tr*e*dici	31	trentuno
14	quatt*o*rdici	32	trentadue
15	qu*i*ndici	33	trentatrè
16	s*e*dici	34	trentaquattro
17	diciassette	40	quaranta
18	diciotto	41	quarantuno
19	diciannove	50	cinquanta
20	venti	60	sessanta
21	ventuno	70	settanta
22	ventidue	80	ottanta
23	ventitrè	90	novanta
30	trenta	100	cento

NOTE.—

(*a*) *Venti* (20), *trenta* (30), *quaranta* (40), and so on up to 100 drop the final vowel when combined with *uno* and *otto*:

e.g. ventuno (21), ventotto (28), trentuno (31), *etc.*

(*b*) The *e* of *tre* (3) when used by itself has no accent but when it is combined with another number a grave accent is placed over it:

e.g. ventitrè, trentatrè, *etc.*

(*c*) *Cento* (100), has no plural form:

e.g. duecento, *two hundred*

(*d*) *Mille* (1,000) has an irregular plural *mila*:

e.g. cinquemila, *five thousand*

(*e*) "One" is not translated before *cento* and *mille*:

e.g. milleseicentoquaranta, *one thousand six hundred and forty*

"And" is not translated between numbers.

(*f*) *Un milione* (plural *milioni*) (1,000,000).
Insert the preposition *di* or *d'* after *milione* when a noun follows:

e.g. un milione d'abitanti, *one million inhabitants*

Dates

In Italian the cardinal numbers are used to express the days of the month, with the exception of *primo* (first). "On" and "of" are not translated, and the article *il* (*l'*) is omitted when preceded by the day of the week.

e.g. il primo aprile (il 1° aprile)	*on the first of April*
martedì, due luglio	*Tuesday, July* 2*nd*
l'otto dicembre	*December* 8*th*
il 1900	1900
nel 1944	*in* 1944
nel settembre del 1960	*in September* 1960

Age

Age is expressed by means of the verb *avere*.

e.g. Quanti anni ha Roberto?	*How old is Robert?*
or Che età ha Roberto?	*What age is Robert?*
Ha nove anni.	*He is nine years old.*
Quanti anni ha Lei?	*How old are you?*
Ho diciannove anni.	*I am nineteen years of age.*
Quanti anni ha il padre di Maria?	*How old is Mary's father?*
Ha quarantasette anni.	*He is forty-seven.*

VOCABULARY

il vill*a*ggio	village	fresco	fresh, cool
la collina	hill	freddo	cold
la montagna	mountain	profondo	deep
il bosco	wood	alto	high
il lago	lake	basso	low
il temporale	storm	diff*i*cile	difficult
il piacere	pleasure, favour	f*a*cile	easy
il sentiero	path, footpath	di s*o*lito	usually
l'ombra	shade	ogni	each, every
all'ombra	in the shade	durare molto	to last a long time
la cartolina	postcard		
la fine	end	cambiare	to change
l'anno bisestile	leap year	diventare	to become
la parola	word	camminare	to walk
la data	date	preferire	to prefer
la p*a*gina	page	nuotare	to swim
il n*u*mero	number	mandare	to send

LA MONTAGNA

L'*a*ria di montagna è fresca e sana. Alcune fam*i*glie prefer*i*scono la montagna al mare. Ci sono dei p*i*ccoli villaggi, delle colline, dei boschi e dei laghi di montagna. L'acqua di questi laghi è molto fredda. Qualche volta ci sono dei temporali, ma, di s*o*lito, non d*u*rano molto. Alla fine d'estate le f*o*glie degli *a*lberi c*a*mbiano colore e div*e*ntano gialle, quasi rosse. Il sole è forte, ma è un piacere camminare nei sentieri dei boschi, all'ombra degli *a*lberi.

EXERCISES

A. Answer in Italian:

1. Parla italiano Lei?
2. Capisce tutte le parole Lei?
3. È diff*i*cile la lingua italiana?
4. Qual è la data di oggi?
5. Quanti giorni ci sono nel mese di settembre?
6. Di che colore sono le f*o*glie in autunno?
7. Cammina molto Lei?
8. Nuota (Lei)?
9. Preferisce il mare alla montagna?
10. Quanti giorni ci sono in un anno bisestile?

B. Translate:

1. On June 1st.
2. On December 11th.

3. There are twenty-eight days in the month of February.
4. There are three hundred and sixty-five days in a year.
5. Today is October 28th.
6. This year is not a leap year.
7. This leaf is nearly yellow.
8. This path is short.
9. These lakes are very deep.
10. These mountains are high.

C. Translate:

1. I speak to her.
2. We speak to him.
3. She speaks to me.
4. You speak to them.
5. We send him a newspaper.
6. She sends us a postcard.
7. I send her a box of handkerchiefs.
8. Maria sends me a letter.
9. The children send us some flowers.
10. You send him a magazine.

D. Translate:

1. Quanti anni ha questo ragazzo?
2. Ha quasi sette anni.
3. Quanti anni ha Lei?
4. Ho diciotto anni.
5. Giovedì, qu*i*ndici maggio.
6. Nel mille novecento quarantasei.
7. Ci sono tre mesi in ogni stagione.
8. Ci sono duecentosei p*a*gine in questo libro.
9. L'It*a*lia ha quasi quarantadue milioni d'abitanti.
10. In un anno bisestile ci sono trecentosessantasei giorni.

E. Translate:

1. This mountain is high.
2. This hill is low.
3. The month of February is short.
4. The air is fresh.
5. Here is a wood.
6. These leaves are nearly yellow.

7. Each season lasts three months.
8. Friday, July 10th, 1959.
9. Four hundred and thirty-eight.
10. Two thousand seven hundred and sixty.

F. Write the present indicative of:

1. *diventare* to become

   io divento,
   tu diventi, *etc.*

2. *credere* to believe

   io credo,
   tu credi, *etc.*

3. *preferire* to prefer

   io preferisco,
   tu preferisci, *etc.*

4. *sentire* to hear

   io sento,
   tu senti, *etc.*

LESSON IX

Reflexive Verbs and Reflexive Pronouns

Reflexive verbs are those whose subject and object are the same person or thing.

e.g. *I* wash *myself*; *she* enjoys *herself*; *it* stops *itself*.

Sometimes a verb is reflexive in Italian and not so in English; these verbs are easy to recognise in Italian as they always have the reflexive pronoun *si* (oneself) appended to the infinitive. Note that the final *-e* of the infinitive is omitted:

e.g.	lavare	*to wash*
	lavarsi	*to wash oneself*
	divertire	*to amuse*
	divertirsi	*to enjoy oneself*

Whereas the reflexive pronoun is often omitted in English, it must always be used in Italian:

e.g.	Io mi preparo.	*I am getting ready.*
	Lei si avvicina alla stazione.	*You are approaching the station.*

NOTE.—Not only the reflexive pronoun *si* but any of the conjunctive pronouns, except *loro* and *Loro*, may thus be appended to the infinitive of a verb:

e.g.	Vado a comprarlo.	*I am going to buy it.*
	Andiamo a vederli.	*We are going to see them.*
	Vado a parlargli.	*I am going to speak to him.*

Here are the reflexive pronouns:

mi	*myself*
ti	*yourself*
si	*himself, herself, itself, yourself*
ci	*ourselves*
vi	*yourself, yourselves*
si	*themselves* (*m.* and *f.*), *yourselves*

Conjugation of Reflexive Verbs

PRESENT INDICATIVE

LAVARSI, *to wash oneself*	DIVERTIRSI, *to enjoy oneself*
io mi lavo	io mi diverto
tu ti lavi	tu ti diverti
egli / ella / Lei } si lava	egli / ella / Lei } si diverte
noi ci laviamo	noi ci divertiamo
voi vi lavate	voi vi divertite
essi / esse / Loro } si l*a*vano	essi / esse / Loro } si div*e*rtono

In the negative and interrogative form of all reflexive verbs *non* is placed before the reflexive pronoun:

e.g. Io non mi diverto. *I am not enjoying myself.*
Non si diverte Lei? *Are you not enjoying yourself?*

Irregular Verbs—*andare, dare, fare, stare*

Having studied the present indicative of the regular verbs ending in *-are*, now let us take the *only* four irregular verbs which end in *-are*.

andare *to go* dare *to give* fare *to make, do*
stare *to be (a temporary condition, health); to stay, remain*

PRESENT INDICATIVE

ANDARE *to go*	DARE *to give*	FARE *to make, do*	STARE *to be, stay*
vado	do	faccio	sto
vai	dai	fai	stai
va	dà	fa	sta
andiamo	diamo	facciamo	stiamo
andate	date	fate	state
vanno	danno	fanno	stanno

NOTE.—The third person singular of the verb *dare* has a grave accent over the vowel; and in the third person plural note the *-anno* in all four verbs.

The Conjunctive Pronoun *ne*

Another conjunctive pronoun to be studied is *ne*, meaning "some, any, some of it, any of it" *when referring to a substantive previously mentioned.* Used as an adverb, *ne* means "from there".

e.g. Ha dei libri Lei ? Sì, ne ho molti.
Have you any books? Yes, I have many (of them).
Ha delle penne Maria? Sì, ne ha due.
Has Mary any pens? Yes, she has two (of them).

In English *of them* is understood, but *ne* must not be omitted in an Italian sentence when an adjective of quantity or a number follows the verb.

NOTE.—The pronouns *lo*, *la*, *li*, *le* and *ne* are appended to the interjection *ecco* (here is, here are, there is, there are):

e.g.	eccolo	*here he (it) is*
	eccola	*here she (it) is*
	eccoli	*here they are (m.)*
	eccole	*here they are (f.)*
	eccone	*here are some (of them)* or *here is some (of it)*

VOCABULARY

l'incontro	meeting	l'orol*o*gio	watch or clock
la vetrina	shop window	il genitore	parent
la c*o*mpera	purchase	la biblioteca	library
il guanto	glove	la borsa	bag, purse
il colletto	collar	nuovo	new
la sciarpa	scarf	poi	then
il prezzo	price	puro	pure
l'art*i*colo	article	verso	towards
il n*a*ilon	nylon	insieme	together
la seta	silk	davanti a	in front of
l'uscita	exit	tutt'e due	both
l'entrata	entrance	(*or* tutti e due)	
il ristorante	restaurant	tutt'e quattro	all four

ammalato	ill
alzarsi	to get up
desiderare	to want
incontrare	to meet
fermare / fermarsi	to stop
conversare	to chat
riposarsi	to rest
fare delle c*o*mpere	to do some shopping
fare colazione	to have lunch
fare una passeggiata	to go for a walk
finire	to finish
*es*cono (*from* uscire, *irr.*)	they go out
mentre	while, whilst
quando	when
Caterina	Catherine
Margherita	Margaret

UN INCONTRO

Anna incontra un'amica, Maria, in città e tutt'e due fanno delle c*o*mpere insieme. Si f*e*rmano davanti ad un neg*o*zio per alcuni minuti. Nella vetrina di questo neg*o*zio v*e*dono guanti, colletti e sciarpe, ma non c'è il prezzo di questi art*i*coli. Le due signorine *e*ntrano nel neg*o*zio e dom*a*ndano il prezzo delle sciarpe. Anna des*i*dera una sciarpa verde, di n*a*ilon, Maria ne des*i*dera una celeste, di seta pura. Le c*o*mprano, poi vanno verso l'uscita. Mentre *e*scono inc*o*ntrano due altre amiche, Caterina e Margherita, conv*e*rsano un poco insieme, poi vanno tutt'e quattro in un ristorante a fare colazione.

EXERCISES

A. Answer the following:

1. Dove vanno Anna e Maria?
2. Dove si f*e*rmano?
3. Che c'è nella vetrina?
4. Ci sono i prezzi degli art*i*coli?
5. Che fanno le signorine?
6. Che compra Anna?
7. Che compra Maria?
8. Preferisce Lei il n*a*ilon alla seta?
9. Chi inc*o*ntrano quando *e*scono dal neg*o*zio?
10. Dove vanno tutt'e quattro?

B. Replace the infinitive by the correct form of the present indicative of each verb:

1. Questa ragazza (alzarsi) di buon'ora.
2. Rosa (comprare) molte cose.

3. Noi (divertirsi) molto.
4. Loro (ric*e*vere) una l*e*ttera.
5. Io (finire) la lezione.
6. Lei (divertirsi) oggi.
7. Carlo (avere) dei libri.
8. Giovanni e Roberto (*e*ssere) contenti.
9. Anna e Caterina (parlare) italiano.
10. Maria (capire) questa lezione.

C. Translate:

1. I have some new gloves. Here they are.
2. Mary has some letters. Here they are.
3. Where are the silk scarves?
4. There they are in the window.
5. Where are you going?
6. What are you doing?
7. How are you, ladies?
8. We are all well, thank you.
9. I stay at home (*a casa*) every Tuesday.
10. These children are not well.

D. Place the reflexive pronoun before the verbs and translate:

1. — diverte
2. — alziamo
3. — div*e*rtono
4. — lavate
5. — *a*lzano
6. — divertite
7. — l*a*vano
8. — alzo
9. — lavi
10. — divertiamo

E. Translate:

1. Questo ragazzo si diverte.
2. Maria non va in città ogni giorno.
3. Questa sciarpa non è di n*a*ilon.
4. Questa lezione non è f*a*cile.
5. Questi ragazzi non stanno bene.
6. Noi ci divertiamo al mare.
7. Anna va spesso ai negozi.
8. Facciamo una passeggiata in campagna.
9. Si diverte Lei, signorina?
10. Sì, gr*a*zie, mi diverto molto.

LESSON X

Possessive Adjectives and Pronouns

Italian uses the possessives both as adjectives and as pronouns. They are usually preceded by the definite article, and they agree with the thing or person possessed, not with the possessor as in English.

e.g.				
e.g.	il mio libro	*my book*	il mio	*mine*
	i miei libri	*my books*	i miei	*mine*
	la sua penna	*his* or *her pen*	la sua	*his* or *hers*
	le sue penne	*his* or *her pens*	le sue	*his* or *hers*

MASCULINE		FEMININE		MEANING	
singular	plural	singular	plural	adjective	pronoun
il mio	i miei	la mia	le mie	*my*	*mine*
il tuo	i tuoi	la tua	le tue	*your*	*yours*
il suo	i suoi	la sua	le sue	*his, her, its*	*his, hers, its*
il Suo	i Suoi	la Sua	le Sue	*your*	*yours*
il nostro	i nostri	la nostra	le nostre	*our*	*ours*
il vostro	i vostri	la vostra	le vostre	*your*	*yours*
il loro	i loro	la loro	le loro	*their*	*theirs*
il Loro	i Loro	la Loro	le Loro	*your*	*yours*

It will be noticed from the Table, and the examples given, that each possessive has four forms:

Masculine singular	Masculine plural
Feminine singular	Feminine plural

Il suo, la sua, may refer to four persons, *his, her, its* and *your* (polite form, frequently spelt *il Suo*, etc.).

If there is any doubt as to the person referred to, confusion may be avoided by using *di lei* ("of her") or *di lui* ("of him").

e.g. Maria legge il suo giornale. *Mary is reading her newspaper.*

But if we wish to say *Mary is reading his newspaper*, we then translate thus:

Maria legge il giornale di lui.

The article is *not* used before the possessive when it precedes a noun denoting family relationships, provided that:

(*a*) the noun is in the singular
(*b*) the noun is not qualified by an adjective
(*c*) the noun is not a diminutive
(*d*) the possessive is not *loro* or *Loro* (their *or* your)

e.g.	mia madre, mio padre	*my mother, my father*
BUT	la mia buona madre	*my good mother*
	la mia piccola sorella la mia sorellina	*my little sister*
	i miei fratelli	*my brothers*
	il loro padre	*their father*
	la Loro madre	*your mother*

The article should be used when one is speaking of the following relations:

nonno	*grandfather*	nonna	*grandmother*
mamma	*mother*	babbo	*daddy*

The indefinite article may also be used before a possessive:

e.g.	un mio libro	*a book of mine* or *one of my books*
	due miei libri	*two of my books*
	molti miei amici	*many of my friends*

Of is not translated.

Relative Pronouns

The most frequently used relative pronouns in Italian are *che* and *cui*:

che	*who, whom, which, that*
cui	(*to, etc.*) *whom, which*

Both are invariable and both are used for persons or things.

che is used as subject or direct object of a verb; although often omitted in English, it may never be omitted in Italian:

e.g. la signora *che* parla — *the lady who is speaking*
il libro *che* compro — *the book I am buying*

cui is used when the relative is an indirect object or when it is governed by a preposition:

e.g. la signora *a cui* parlo — *the lady to whom I am speaking*
il libro *di cui* parlo — *the book of which I am speaking*

There is also another relative pronoun which refers to persons or things, viz: *il quale* (fem. *la quale*, with the plurals *i quali* and *le quali*). This pronoun is used instead of *che* or *cui* to avoid ambiguity. When *il quale* is governed by a preposition, this preposition and the article combine to form one word as already shown in Lesson VI.

e.g. La sorella del professore, alla quale ho mandato la cartolina.
The professor's sister to whom I sent the postcard.

The relative pronoun *whose* is translated by *il cui, la cui,* etc. The article agrees with the noun which follows:

e.g. Questa ragazza, il cui cane è perduto, è triste.
This girl, whose dog is lost, is sad.

Ordinal Numbers (*continued*)

8th	ottavo	13th	tredic*e*simo, etc.
9th	nono	20th	vent*e*simo
10th	d*e*cimo	21st	ventun*e*simo
11th	undic*e*simo	22nd	ventidu*e*simo
12th	dodic*e*simo	30th	trent*e*simo, etc.

Ordinal numbers, except 1st to 10th, are formed by dropping the final vowel of the cardinal number and adding -*e*simo:

e.g. *u*ndici	11	→	undic*e*simo	11th
d*o*dici	12	→	dodic*e*simo	12th
venti	20	→	vent*e*simo	20th, etc.

but the last vowel of 23, 33, 43, etc., being a stressed vowel, is not omitted:

e.g. ventitrè → ventitre*e*simo
trentatrè → trentatre*e*simo, etc.

From 11th onwards the ordinals may also be translated thus:

11th	d*e*cimo primo
12th	d*e*cimo secondo
13th	d*e*cimo terzo, etc.

Remember that ordinal numbers are adjectives and must agree with the noun:

e.g. il secondo mese	*the second month*
la prima stagione	*the first season*
i primi giorni	*the first days*
le prime settimane	*the first weeks*

Ordinal numbers are used in Italian without the article after names of rulers:

e.g. Enrico quinto	*Henry V*
Pio d*e*cimo	*Pius X*

They are also used after a few words such as *canto*, *capitolo*, *volume*, *lezione*, etc.

e.g. Canto s*e*ttimo	*Canto* 7	Volume secondo	*Volume* 2
Cap*i*tolo quarto	*Chapter* 4	Lezione nona	*Lesson* 9

Fractions

Fractions are formed as in English by using the cardinal numeral as the numerator and the ordinal numeral as the denominator:

e.g. un terzo	*one third*	quattro quinti	*four-fifths*
tre quarti	*three-quarters*		

mezzo (or *mezz'*) "half", when used as an adjective agrees with the noun:

e.g. una mezza bott*i*glia — una mezz'ora

but is usually invariable when the noun comes first:

e.g. una bott*i*glia e mezzo — un'ora e mezzo

NOTE.—The noun "half" is *la metà.*

VOCABULARY

il mercato	market
la dom*e*stica	servant
la macelleria	butcher's shop
il macell*a*io	butcher
il manzo	beef
il vitello	veal, calf
l'agnello	lamb
il pesce	fish
il pesciv*e*ndolo	fishmonger
la s*o*gliola	sole
il merluzzo	cod
la tr*i*glia	mullet
il legume	vegetable
la verdura	green vegetables
il pisello	pea
il fagiolino	French bean
lo zucchino	small marrow
gli spinaci	spinach
il fruttiv*e*ndolo	fruiterer
la frutta (*pl.* le frutta)	fruit
la pera	pear
la mela	apple
la pesca	peach
l'uva	grape, grapes
il melone	melon
il coc*o*mero	water melon
la maced*o*nia di frutta	fruit salad
il (la) nipote	nephew (niece)
l'eserc*i*zio	exercise
qui, qua	here
poi	then
caro	dear, expensive
crudo	raw
cotto	cooked
o	or
o . . . o	either . . . or
ecc*e*tera (*abb.* ecc.)	etcetera (etc.)
gradito	welcome
estivo	summer (*adj.*)
mi dica	tell me
stare a casa	to stay at home
Rosa	Rose
Enrico	Henry

AL MERCATO

Ogni mattina, Rosa, la dom*e*stica della signora Valli, si alza di buon'ora e va al mercato. Vicino al mercato c'è una macelleria dove Rosa compra la carne: manzo, vitello o agnello.

Qu*a*ndo la signora Valli des*i*dera del pesce, Rosa lo compra dal pesciv*e*ndolo: s*o*gliola, merluzzo, tr*i*glia, ecc.

Guarda i prezzi della verdura; piselli, fagiolini, zucchini; poi della frutta: mele, pere, uva, meloni e coc*o*meri.

La frutta è buona per la salute, e non è cara nei mesi estivi: così ogni fam*i*glia ne m*a*ngia molta, o cruda o cotta. La maced*o*nia di frutta è sempre gradita, non è vero?

Ogni dom*e*nica la signora Valli prepara una maced*o*nia di frutta e invita i suoi nipoti a fare colazione.

Buon appetito a tutti!

EXERCISES

A. Answer in Italian:

1. Chi è Rosa?
2. Dove va ogni mattina?
3. Che compra al mercato?
4. M*a*ngia molta carne Lei?
5. Preferisce il pesce?
6. Mi dica i nomi di tre frutta.
7. E i nomi di tre legumi?
8. Dov'è la porta?
9. Dove sono i libri?
10. Dove sono le s*e*die?

B. Translate the word in brackets:

1. Ecco (*my*) giardino.
2. Ecco (*his*) casa.
3. Dov'è (*your*) sorella?
4. Dov'è (*their*) fratello?
5. Ecco (*my*) penna.
6. Ecco (*her*) libro.
7. Dove sono (*your*) genitori?
8. Dove sono (*his*) zii?
9. Queste sono (*her*) sorelle.
10. Questi sono (*my*) fratelli.

C. Translate:

1. The first house.
2. Chapter three.
3. Henry VIII.
4. Volume six.
5. Lesson five.
6. The ladies who are speaking Italian are English.
7. The gentlemen of whom you are speaking are French.
8. The boy to whom I give the book.
9. The girl from whom I receive a letter.
10. The students who are in this classroom.
11. Half of this pear is for you.
12. Thirty minutes make half an hour.

D. Translate:

1. Mio fratello va alla biblioteca.
2. Scrivo l'eserc*i*zio nel mio quaderno.
3. Gli studenti st*u*diano le loro lezioni.
4. Rispondo alla l*e*ttera di mia madre.
5. Scrivo una cartolina alla mia amica.
6. Io sto bene ma mia sorella è ammalata.
7. Il fratello del mio amico è al mare.
8. I miei genitori stanno bene.
9. Ecco l'orol*o*gio di mio padre.
10. Ecco la borsa di mia madre.

E. Translate:

1. I am not going to the market.
2. My father is going to town.
3. Margaret is not here today.
4. How are you, Charles and Robert?
5. We are very well, thank you.
6. My sister is not well.
7. My brothers are in the country.
8. Our friends are at the seaside.
9. Have you any brothers, Mary?
10. Yes, I have two brothers and three sisters.

REVISION TEST

A. Translate and put into the plural:

1. The book
2. The door
3. The idea
4. The uncle
5. The lesson
6. The garden
7. The window
8. The name
9. The student (*m.*)
10. The student (*f.*)

B. Complete with a suitable noun:

1. Il —— italiano
2. La —— francese
3. I —— inglesi
4. Le —— gialle
5. I —— rossi
6. L' —— italiana
7. Le —— tedesche
8. I —— tedeschi
9. Molti —— lunghi
10. Molte —— lunghe

C. Translate:

1. Mary and John have many friends.
2. Ann and Robert are Italian.
3. Margaret and Charles speak French.
4. We receive a postcard.
5. You receive a letter.
6. The children are well.
7. I do not understand every word.
8. We understand this lesson because it is easy.

D. Answer in Italian:

1. Come sta, signorina (*o* signore)?
2. Dov'è il Suo quaderno?
3. Qual è il terzo mese dell'anno?
4. Qual è la quarta stagione dell'anno?
5. Di che colore è l'erba?
6. Di che colore è Suo dizion*a*rio?
7. Capisce (Lei) questa lezione?
8. Cap*i*scono (Loro) tutte le parole?
9. Quanto fanno tr*e*dici più due?
10. Quanto fanno diciannove meno tre?

E. Translate:

1. In the box
2. On the tree
3. For the lady
4. In the garden
5. At the house
6. With the student
7. From the friend (*m.*)
8. Of the uncle
9. To the student (*f.*)
10. Of the master

F. Put the answers to Exercise E into the plural.

G. Write in letters:

28, 35, 49, 52, 69, 100, 460, 1000, 5800, 1,000,000, $\frac{2}{3}$, $\frac{1}{4}$, $\frac{3}{4}$, $\frac{1}{5}$.

H. Translate:

1. On the 6th of May
2. On the 1st of July
3. In 1949
4. The third house
5. The seventh day

I. Complete with a suitable adjective:

1. I ragazzi sono ——
2. Le ragazze sono ——
3. Questo giardino è ——
4. Questa casa è ——
5. Questi signori sono ——

J. Translate:

1. I see the master, I see him.
2. We see the mistress, we see her.
3. Mary speaks to him.
4. John speaks to her.
5. The teachers speak to us.

SECTION TWO

LESSON XI

Formation of the Past Participle

To form the past participles of regular and some irregular verbs, change the infinitive endings as follows:

-are to *-ato* *-ere* to *-uto* *-ire* to *-ito*

e.g.	parlare, parlato	potere (*irr.*), potuto
	vendere, venduto	uscire (*irr.*), uscito
	capire, capito	

Note that the characteristic *e* of the verbs in the second conjugation has changed to *u.*

The compound tenses are formed by using one of the auxiliary verbs *avere* or *essere* together with the past participle. *Avere* is used in conjugating all transitive and some intransitive verbs.[1]

Perfect Tense

	PARLARE, *to speak*		
ho	parlato	(*I spoke,*	Similarly:
hai	,,	*I have spoken,*	VENDERE, ho venduto, *etc.*
ha	,,	etc.)	CAPIRE, ho capito, *etc.*
abbiamo	,,		
avete	,,		
hanno	,,		

Use of the Perfect Tense

The perfect tense expresses an action which happened in the past but has reference to the present, or an action whose effects are still lasting:

e.g. Roberto ha venduto la casa.
Robert has sold the house.
Oggi non ho ricevuto una lettera.
I did not receive a letter today.

[1] Transitive verbs are those which take an object, e.g. *comprare*, *vendere*, etc. Intransitive verbs are those used without an object, e.g. *arrivare*, *restare*, etc.

Disjunctive Pronouns

me	*me*
te	*you*
lui *or* esso	*him, it*
lei *or* essa	*her, it*
Lei	*you*
sè	*himself, herself, itself, themselves*
noi	*us*
voi	*you*
loro *or* essi	*them*
loro *or* esse	*them*
Loro	*you*

These pronouns, except *lui*, *lei*, *loro* when used as emphatic subject pronouns (e.g. *lui* dice che, *he* says that . . ., *loro* dicono che, *they* say that . . .) usually follow the verb and are often separated from it by a preposition.

They are most commonly used:

(*a*) after prepositions:

e.g. Ecco una lettera per me. *Here is a letter for me.*
Vado con lui. *I am going with him.*

(*b*) when a verb has two direct or indirect objects:

e.g. Abbiamo veduto te e lei oggi.
We saw (*have seen*) *you and her today.*
Parliamo a Lei ed a lui.
We are speaking to you and to him.

(*c*) for emphasis:

e.g. Questa cartolina è per loro, non per noi.
This postcard is for them, not for us.

Time—*l'ora*

In Italian the definite article precedes the hour:

e.g. Che ora è? *or* Che ore sono?	*What time is it?*
È l'una.	*It is one o'clock.*
Sono le due.	*It is two o'clock.*

è is used only with one o'clock, midday and midnight; *sono* is used with all the other hours.

e.g. È mezzogiorno.	*It is midday, noon.*
È mezzanotte.	*It is midnight.*
BUT Sono le tre.	*It is three o'clock.*
Sono le otto.	*It is eight o'clock.*

NOTE.—Both the articles and the verb agree: in *è l'una*, *sono le due*, etc., the articles are feminine singular *or* feminine plural, the words *ora* and *ore* being understood.

alle tre e un quarto	*at* 3.15 *a.m.*
alle tre meno un quarto	*at* 2.45 *a.m.*
alle otto e mezzo	*at* 8.30 *a.m.*
alle nove e venti	*at* 9.20 *a.m.*

The twenty-four hour system is used in Italy in official language, e.g. times of trains, theatre performances, etc., hence 4 p.m. is translated *sedici*, at 11 p.m. *alle ventitrè*.

e.g. Il treno arriva alle diciannove e dieci.
The train arrives at 7.10 *p.m.*

VOCABULARY

il teatro	theatre	il violoncello	cello
la giornata	day (*the whole day*)	il tenore	tenor
		il soprano	soprano
la festa	feast, rejoicing	il basso	bass
l'onom*a*stico	saint's day *or* name day	il bis	encore
		bis	twice
il compleanno	birthday	bravo	clever, able
il biglietto	ticket	vero	true, real
il posto	seat *or* place	suonare *or* sonare	to play (*an instrument*)
l'*o*pera	opera		
il secondo	second	giocare	to play (*a game*)
il sil*e*nzio	silence	guardare attorno	to look around
il Direttore d'Orchestra	the conductor	potere (*irr.*)	to be able
la direzione	direction	uscire (*irr.*)	to go out
la sorpresa	surprise	salutare	to greet
lo strumento	instrument	chiamare	to call
il pianoforte	piano	già	already
il violino	violin		

AL TEATRO

Oggi è una bella giornata per Maria Bertipacini perchè è il suo onom*a*stico. I suoi genitori hanno comprato i biglietti per l'*o*pera, e hanno invitato Margherita, l'amica della loro f*i*glia. Alle venti, tutti e quattro vanno insieme al teatro. L'*o*pera com*i*ncia alle venti e quaranta, e finisce a mezzanotte.

Eccoli ora ai loro posti; gu*a*rdano attorno alla vasta sala, vedono amici e li sal*u*tano. L'*o*pera che danno è *La Norma* di Vincenzo Bellini.

Dopo alcuni secondi di sil*e*nzio, l'orchestra, sotto la direzione del direttore, com*i*ncia a suonare. I genitori di Maria hanno già sentito quest'*o*pera ma per Maria e la sua amica è una vera e bella sorpresa.

EXERCISES

A. Answer the following:

1. Chi ha comprato i biglietti per l'*o*pera?
2. Perchè?
3. Come si chiama l'amica di Maria?
4. Dove vanno tutti e quattro?
5. Quale *o*pera vanno a vedere?
6. Di chi è quest'*o*pera?
7. Chi ha già veduto *La Norma*?
8. Ha Lei veduto un'*o*pera italiana?
9. Canta Lei?
10. Suona uno strumento?
11. A che ora com*i*ncia l'*o*pera?
12. E a che ora finisce?

B. Give the past participle of:

1. finire
2. cantare
3. partire
4. ric*e*vere
5. potere
6. suonare
7. v*e*ndere
8. servire
9. cr*e*dere
10. giocare

C. Translate:

1. I have not bought the tickets for them.
2. We have sold the house to you, not to him.
3. Robert has received a letter today from her.
4. Charles and Peter received a postcard from us.
5. I have finished my lunch.
6. This child has not understood the opera.
7. Have you (*pl.*) heard this tenor?
8. These children have spoken Italian all day to me.
9. Mario has bought a piano.
10. My mother has invited some friends.

D. Translate:

1. La signora apre il libro e lo legge.
2. Il signore compra un'automobile per loro.
3. Noi abbiamo ricevuto due cartoline da lui.
4. Marherita ha suonato il violino per noi.
5. Il mio onomastico è il 15 agosto.
6. Ma il mio compleanno è il 6 ottobre.
7. Questo direttore d'orchestra è molto bravo.
8. Chi ha sentito quest'opera?

LESSON XII

Past Participles (*continued*)

The past participle of *avere* is *avuto*, and that of *essere* is *stato*. As already stated, *avere* is used to form the compound tenses of all transitive and some intransitive verbs. *Essere* is used with most intransitive verbs, all reflexive verbs and the verb *essere* itself.[1]

NOTE.—The past participles of verbs conjugated with *essere* (apart from reflexive verbs) always agree with the subject in gender and number:

e.g. Il ragazzo è arrivato.	*The boy has arrived.*
La ragazza è arrivata.	*The girl has arrived.*
I ragazzi sono arrivati.	*The boys have arrived.*
Le ragazze sono arrivate.	*The girls have arrived.*

When the verb is conjugated with *avere*, the past participle may or may not agree with its direct object. It does not agree when the object follows the verb; it usually agrees when the object precedes the verb; it must always agree when the direct personal pronoun precedes the verb.

e.g. Abbiamo comprato una casa. *We have bought a house.*
Ecco la casa che abbiamo comprata (*or* comprato).
Here is the house we have bought.
L'abbiamo comprata. *We have bought it.*

[1] The following are examples of verbs conjugated with *essere* in the compound tenses. Note that many of these are verbs of motion.

andare	*to go*	partire	*to depart*
arrivare	*to arrive*	restare	*to remain, stay*
cadere	*to fall*	rimanere (*p.p.* rimasto)	*to remain*
diventare	*to become*	salire	*to go up*
entrare	*to enter*	scendere (*p.p.* sceso)	*to descend*
morire (*p.p.* morto)	*to die*	uscire	*to go out*
nascere (*p.p.* nato)	*to be born*	venire (*p.p.* venuto)	*to come*

The past participle may be used adjectivally, in which case it is known as a verbal adjective. It then follows the same rules of agreement as an adjective:

e.g. le vacanze passate a Roma	*the holidays spent in Rome*
i libri scritti dal Manzoni	*the books written by Manzoni*

Perfect Tense of the Auxiliaries

AVERE		ESSERE	
ho avuto	*I have had,*	sono stato (a)	*I have been,*
hai avuto	etc.	sei stato (a)	etc.
ha avuto		è stato (a)	
abbiamo avuto		siamo stati (e)	
avete avuto		siete stati (e)	
hanno avuto		sono stati (e)	

Perfect Tense of Reflexive Verbs

LAVARSI, *to wash oneself*

mi sono lavato (a)	*I washed* (*myself*), etc.
ti sei lavato (a)	
si è lavato (a)	Similarly:
ci siamo lavati (e)	DIVERTIRSI, *to enjoy oneself:*
vi siete lavati (e)	mi sono divertito (a), *etc.*
si sono lavati (e)	

The past participle of reflexive verbs usually agrees with the direct object.

In the negative and the interrogative forms *non* precedes the reflexive pronoun:

e.g. Non mi sono divertito (a). *I did not enjoy myself*, etc.
Non ti sei divertito (a).
Non si è divertito (a).
Non ci siamo divertiti (e).
Non vi siete divertiti (e).
Non si sono divertiti (e).
Non mi sono divertito (a) io? *Did I not enjoy myself*, etc.
Non ci siamo divertiti (e) noi? *etc.*

Position of Adjectives (*continued*)

Most adjectives, as already stated in Lesson III, follow the noun they qualify. There are, however, adjectives of common use which usually precede the noun, unless they are modified by an adverb or used emphatically. Here is a list of these adjectives.

bello	*beautiful*	lungo	*long*
brutto	*ugly*	corto, breve	*short*
grande	*big*	gi*o*vane	*young*
p*i*ccolo	*small, little*	vecchio	*old*
buono	*good*	ricco	*rich*
cattivo	*bad, naughty*	p*o*vero	*poor*
santo	*holy*		

Some adjectives vary in meaning according to their position:

e.g. un grand'uomo	*a great man*
BUT un uomo grande	*a tall man*
una p*o*vera donna	*an unfortunate woman*
BUT una donna p*o*vera	*a poor woman*

Irregular Adjectives

The adjectives

bello	*beautiful, lovely, fine*
buono	*good*
grande	*big, great*
santo	*saint*

undergo various changes when they precede the noun.

Bello has similar forms to the definite article:

e.g. un bel cavallo	*a beautiful horse*
una bella rosa	*a beautiful rose*
un bell'*a*lbero	*a lovely tree*
una bell'*i*sola	*a beautiful island*
un bello sp*e*cchio	*a lovely mirror*
due bei bambini	*two beautiful children*
due belle rose	*two beautiful roses*
due begli *a*lberi	*two lovely trees*

Buono in the singular has forms similar to those of the indefinite article, but it is quite regular in the plural forms:

e.g. un buon ragazzo	*a good boy*
una buona ragazza	*a good girl*
una buon'amica	*a good friend* (*f.*)
un buon amico	*a good friend* (*m.*)
un buono stip*e*ndio	*a good salary*
BUT due buoni ragazzi	*two good boys*

Grande and *santo* become *gran* and *san* before a masculine noun in the singular beginning with any consonant except *s* impure or *z*, in which case its full form is kept. They become *grand'* and *sant'* before a noun beginning with a vowel:

e.g. un gran favore	*a great favour*
un grande scrittore	*a great writer*
un grand'*a*lbero	*a large tree*
una grand'*e*poca	*a great epoch*
Sant'Ant*o*nio	*St. Anthony*
San Pietro	*St. Peter*
Santo St*e*fano	*St. Stephen*
Sant'Anna	*St. Anne*

Santo, however, is not irregular when it means "holy" or "blessed":

e.g. il santo Padre — *the Holy Father* (*the Pope*)

D*i*sputano tutto il santo giorno.
They argue the whole blessed day.

NOTE.—These adjectives are always written in their full form when they come after the noun they qualify or are separated from it.

e.g. Ecco un bel duomo.	*Here is a beautiful cathedral.*
BUT Questo duomo è bello.	*This cathedral is beautiful.*
Questo duomo è molto bello.	*This cathedral is very beautiful.*

VOCABULARY

il podere	farm	l'oca	goose
al podere	on the farm	l'*a*nitra	duck
il parente	relation	il gallo	cock
il marito	husband	la gallina	hen
la m*o*glie	wife	il pulcino	chick
il cognato	brother-in-law	il con*i*glio	rabbit
la cognata	sister-in-law	la partenza	departure
il (la) cugino (-a)	cousin	l'animale dom*e*stico	domestic animal
il contadino	peasant, farm worker	ogni tanto	every now and again
il cavallo	horse		
il cane	dog	mentre	while, whilst
il gatto	cat	dappertutto	everywhere
la stalla	cow-shed	conversare	to converse, chat
il bue, *pl.* buoi	ox, *pl.* oxen	seguire	to follow
la mucca	cow	il campo	field
il maiale	pig	la legna	firewood
il mulo	mule	aiutare	to help
l'*a*sino	ass, donkey	notare	to note

AL PODERE

Il signor Moscari, fratello del padre di Carlo, *a*bita in campagna con sua m*o*glie e i loro due figli Roberto e Pietro. Hanno un podere, e ogni tanto Carlo ed i suoi genitori p*a*ssano una giornata con i loro parenti. Mentre la madre di Carlo conversa con la sua cognata e il padre v*i*sita il podere, i tre ragazzi si div*e*rtono insieme. I due cani, Pilù e Buffi, li s*e*guono dappertutto. A questo podere ci sono oche, *a*nitre, galline, pulcini, conigli e gatti. I ragazzi v*i*sitano le stalle dove sono le mucche, poi v*e*dono i maiali. N*o*tano i buoi che lav*o*rano nei campi ed i muli che p*o*rtano la legna. P*a*rlano con i contadini che inc*o*ntrano. Che bella giornata! Carlo è sempre un po' triste quando arriva l'ora della partenza per la città.

EXERCISES

A. Answer in Italian:

1. Chi è il signor Moscari?
2. *A*bita in città?
3. Come si chi*a*mano i suoi due *fi*gli?

4. Dove p*a*ssano una giornata, ogni tanto, Carlo e i suoi genitori?
5. Che fa la madre di Carlo?
6. Che fa suo padre?
7. Che fanno i tre ragazzi?
8. Chi lavora bene nei campi?
9. Ha (Lei) capito bene questa lezione?
10. Chi ha capito ogni parola?

B. (*a*) Put the correct form of *buono* in front of the following nouns:

1. —— amico
2. —— amici
3. —— amica
4. —— amiche
5. —— podere

(*b*) Put the correct form of *grande* in front of the following:

1. Il —— edif*i*cio
2. La —— sala
3. Un —— vi*a*ggio
4. Una —— biblioteca
5. Due —— uccelli

C. Translate:

1. We do not live in the country.
2. Robert's father has a farm.
3. He has horses, cows, pigs and many other domestic animals.
4. This little dog follows me everywhere.
5. This donkey is called Morella.
6. There are many rabbits on this farm.
7. The children enjoyed themselves.
8. They have helped their father.
9. They got up early this morning.
10. The peasants have worked well today.

D. (*a*) Complete with the correct form of *bello*:

1. Un —— cielo
2. Una —— bambina
3. Dei —— fiori
4. Delle —— rose
5. Un —— uccello

(*b*) Complete with the correct form of *santo*:

1. —— Rita
2. —— Giuseppe
3. —— Ant*o*nio
4. —— St*e*fano
5. —— Elisabetta

E. Translate the words in brackets:

1. I cavalli (*that*) vediamo.
2. La ragazza (*who*) lavora bene.
3. Lo zio (*with whom*) parliamo.
4. I fiori (*that*) vedo.
5. La contadina (*of whom*) p*a*rlano.
6. L'uccello (*that*) guardo.
7. La zia (*from whom*) ho ricevuto la l*e*ttera.
8. La signora (*to whom*) ho mandato una cartolina.
9. I ragazzi (*who*) *a*bitano in campagna.
10. I cani (*that*) sono davanti alla porta.

F. Write in full the perfect tense of the following verbs:

parlare ric*e*vere partire

Il Secondo Gioco dell'Alfabeto

This time the definitions are in Italian, but the answers to the definitions will be in alphabetical order:

1. L'ottavo mese dell'anno a......
2. Il contr*a*rio di *alto* b......
3. Un n*u*mero cardinale c......
4. Una chiesa importante d......
5. Una stagione dell'anno e......
6. Il contr*a*rio di *difficile* f......
7. Nome di un ragazzo g......
8. Gli abitanti d'It*a*lia i......
9. Il contr*a*rio di *corto* l......
10. Nome di una ragazza m......
11. Un n*u*mero ordinale n......
12. Il d*e*cimo mese dell'anno o......
13. Una stagione dell'anno p......
14. Quanto fanno trenta più dieci? q......
15. Un fiore r......
16. Un giorno della settimana s......
17. Quanti giorni ci sono nel mese d'aprile? t......
18. Quanto fanno s*e*dici meno cinque? u......
19. Un colore v......
20. Un parente z......

LESSON XIII

Demonstrative Adjectives

There are three demonstrative adjectives:

Questo this
Codesto, also written *cotesto*, that
Quello that

Questo usually refers to somebody or something near the person who is speaking.
Codesto refers to somebody or something near the person spoken to (but it is rarely used nowadays).
Quello refers to somebody or something far from both the person who is speaking and the person spoken to.

Questo and *codesto* drop the final vowel and take the apostrophe before a noun in the singular beginning with a vowel.

e.g.	questo libro	*this book*
	quest'alunno (alunna)	*this pupil*
	codesto quaderno	*that exercise book*
	codest'inchiostro	*that ink*

Quello has various forms similar to those of the definite article and the adjective *bello* (see Lesson XII):

e.g.	quel ragazzo	*that boy*
	quella ragazza	*that girl*
	quell'alunno (alunna)	*that pupil*
	quello studente	*that student*
	quei libri	*those books*
	quelle signore	*those ladies*
	quegli alunni / quelle alunne	*those pupils*
	quegli studenti	*those students*
	quegli zii	*those uncles*

Irregular Verbs—*tenere, dire*

It may interest students to know that there are approximately 7000 verbs in Italian, more than 5000 of which end in *-are*. As already stated, there are only four irregular verbs ending in *-are*, viz:

andare	*to go, p.p.* andato
dare	*to give, p.p.* dato
fare	*to do, make, p.p.* fatto
stare	*to be, stay, p.p.* stato

Having studied the present indicative of the four irregular verbs ending in *-are* (see page 67), now let us study some in *-ere* and *-ire*.

PRESENT INDICATIVE

TENERE, *to hold* (*p.p.* tenuto)	DIRE, *to say, tell* (*p.p.* detto)
tengo	dico
tieni	dici
tiene	dice
teniamo	diciamo
tenete	dite
tengono	d*i*cono

Many of the irregular verbs ending in *-ere* and *-ire* are only irregular in certain tenses.

The verbs *leggere*, to read; *scrivere*, to write; *aprire*, to open and *chiudere*, to shut, are quite regular in the present tense, but have very irregular past participles:

leggere,	*p.p.* letto
scr*i*vere,	*p.p.* scritto
aprire,	*p.p.* aperto
chi*u*dere,	*p.p.* chiuso

All these verbs except *andare* and *stare* are conjugated with *avere* in the compound tenses.

e.g. Sono andato a casa ed ho letto un libro.
I went home and read a book.
Ho scritto la lettera e ne sono stato contento.
I wrote the letter and was pleased with it.

VOCABULARY

il Lago Maggiore	Lake Maggiore	lontano da	far from
il Lago di Como	Lake Como	numeroso	numerous
il Lago di Garda	Lake Garda	specialmente	especially
la veduta	view	forte	strong, bright
la gita, il giro	tour, excursion	profondo	deep
il vaporetto	steamer	prefer*i*bile	preferable
la m*a*cchina, l'autom*o*bile	car	che . . .!	what a . . .!
in m*a*cchina	by car	quanti(e)! (*in exclamations*)	what a lot of . . .!
il pullman, il torpedone	coach, touring car	spl*e*ndere	to shine
in pullman, in torpedone	by coach	l*e*ggere (*p.p.* letto)	to read
la galleria	tunnel, arcade	scr*i*vere (*p.p.* scritto)	to write
la luce	light	dire (*p.p.* detto)	to say, tell
il cielo	sky	aprire (*p.p.* aperto)	to open
il caldo, il calore	heat	tenere (*p.p.* tenuto)	to hold
il tramonto	sunset	chi*u*dere (*p.p.* chiuso)	to shut, close
il pomer*i*ggio	afternoon	si (*pron. indef.*)	one, people, they
la sera	evening	attraverso	through
stasera	this evening		
intorno a	around		

I LAGHI

In It*a*lia ci sono molti bei laghi, grandi e p*i*ccoli. Non lontano da Milano i tre laghi più importanti si chi*a*mano Lago Maggiore, Lago di Como, e Lago di Garda. La veduta delle montagne intorno al Lago di Garda è magn*i*fica. Si fanno belle gite con il vaporetto sul lago, o in autom*o*bile sulla strada attraverso le numerose gallerie. Quanti bei giardini con begli *a*lberi e fiori di molti colori! La luce è forte, il bel sole splende nel cielo azzurro ed è un piacere *e*ssere vicino all'*a*cqua. Molti fanno gite in torpedone. Con il gran caldo che fa nei mesi estivi è sempre prefer*i*bile partire la mattina di buon'ora, riposarsi durante le ore calde del pomer*i*ggio e ritornare la sera. Spesso ci sono tramonti magn*i*fici, specialmente nei mesi di agosto e di settembre. Siamo sempre contenti di vedere un bel tramonto.

EXERCISES

A. Translate the reading passage *I Laghi.*

B. Translate:

1. That lake is deep.
2. These steamers are not very big.
3. We have seen many beautiful flowers.
4. The sunset is beautiful this evening.
5. Have you seen Lake Garda?
6. No, but I have been to Lake Maggiore.
7. Today we are going to Lake Como.
8. It is a pleasure to visit the three lakes.
9. What a blue sky!
10. What a lot of tunnels!
11. That rose, near you, is beautiful.
12. The light is not bright today.

C. Give the third person singular of the present and perfect tense of the following verbs:

1. andare
2. dare
3. fare
4. stare
5. l*e*ggere
6. scr*i*vere
7. dire
8. aprire
9. tenere
10. finire

D. Translate:

1. Il sole è stato forte oggi.
2. Il tramonto è magn*i*fico stasera.
3. Ho fatto una gita in pullman.
4. Dov'è stato Lei?
5. Intorno al lago.
6. Ha (Lei) letto il giornale?
7. Sì, l'ho letto questo pomer*i*ggio.
8. Carlo ha scritto tre cartoline.
9. Caterina ha aperto la finestra.
10. Noi abbiamo dato la l*e*ttera alla signora.
11. Che cosa ha detto Maria?
12. Che cosa ha detto, Maria?

E. Answer the following twenty questions on grammar:

1. How many letters are there in the Italian alphabet?
2. How many genders are there?
3. How do masculine nouns ending *-o* and *-e* form their plurals?
4. How do masculine nouns ending in *-io* form their plurals? Give examples.
5. What are the different forms of the definite article?
6. What are the different forms of the indefinite article?
7. How many forms has an adjective ending in *-o*? Give examples.
8. How many forms has an adjective ending in *-e*? Give examples.
9. How do nouns and adjectives ending in *-co* and *-go* form their plurals? Give examples.
10. How many conjugations of verbs are there in Italian? Give an example of each.
11. Is the present indicative of verbs ending in *-ire* the same for all verbs?
12. Name the subject pronouns.
13. In Italian are the subject pronouns always expressed?
14. Give all the contracted forms of the prepositions *da* and the definite article.
15. Which two prepositions are used separately, or may only be contracted with *il* and *i*?
16. Name the masculine possessive adjectives and pronouns in the singular and plural.
17. Name the feminine possessive adjectives and pronouns in the singular and plural.
18. Name the reflexive pronouns, and two reflexive verbs.
19. How are the past participles of regular verbs formed?
20. Name the only four irregular verbs ending in *-are*.

LESSON XIV

Future Tense

To form the future tense, and the conditional which will be studied later, certain endings are added to the infinitive less the final vowel. Regular verbs ending in *-are* undergo a slight change, viz. the *a* of the infinitive ending is changed to *e*. The endings of the future tense of all verbs, regular and irregular, are the same, and are as follows:

First person singular	-ò
Second person singular	-ai
Third person singular	-à
First person plural	-emo
Second person plural	-ete
Third person plural	-anno

Note the grave accent on the First and Third persons singular.

Now let us study the future tense of the three model verbs.

FUTURE TENSE

PARLARE		VENDERE	
parlerò	*I shall* or *will*	venderò	*I shall* or *will*
parlerai	*speak*, etc.	venderai	*sell*, etc.
parlerà		venderà	
parleremo		venderemo	
parlerete		venderete	
parleranno		venderanno	

CAPIRE	
capirò	*I shall* or *will understand*, etc.
capirai	
capirà	
capiremo	
capirete	
capiranno	

Some verbs have a slight irregularity in the future (and conditional) tense:

	andare	*to go*	andrò
	vedere	*to see*	vedrò
	potere	*to be able*	potrò
also	avere	*to have*	avrò

Essere is very irregular; it changes the stem completely and becomes *sarò* (see below).

The other three irregular verbs in *-are* do not change the letter *a* to *e*:

dare	*to give*	darò
fare	*to do, make*	farò
stare	*to be*	starò

Future Tense of the Auxiliaries

AVERE		ESSERE	
avrò	*I shall* or *will*	sarò	*I shall* or *will*
avrai	*have*, etc.	sarai	*be*, etc.
avrà		sarà	
avremo		saremo	
avrete		sarete	
avranno		saranno	

Use of the Future Tense

(*a*) As in English, it is used to denote what is going to happen. Whereas in English the future idea is often conveyed by the present tense, in Italian the future tense must be used.

e.g. *When I am rich, I shall buy a beautiful house.*
Quando sarò ricco, comprerò una bella casa.
If Charles writes to me at the end of the month I will reply to him.
Se Carlo mi scriverà alla fine del mese io gli risponderò.

(Note, however, the conversational *Ci vado stasera.*)

(*b*) It is used to express what is probable:

e.g. *This coffee is too strong* (*probably*) *for you, Charles.*
Questo caffè sarà troppo forte per te, Carlo.

Irregular Verbs—*potere, volere, venire*

PRESENT INDICATIVE

POTERE, *to be able*, *p.p.* potuto

posso *I am able, I can, I may*, etc.
puoi
può
possiamo
potete
possono

Note the grave accent on the third person singular.

VOLERE, *to want*, *to be willing*, *p.p.* voluto

voglio *I want, I am willing*, etc.
vuoi
vuole (*or* vuol)
vogliamo
volete
vogliono

NOTE.—The *e* in *vuole* may be omitted:

e.g. Vuole (*or* vuol) venire con me?
Do you want to come with me?
Vuol aspettarmi un momento?
Will you wait for me a moment?
Egli vuol stare a casa.
He wants to stop at home.

The future of *volere* is *vorrò*, *vorrai*, etc.

VENIRE, *to come*, *p.p.* venuto

vengo *I come, I am coming*, etc.
vieni
viene
veniamo
venite
vengono

The future of *venire* is *verrò*, *verrai*, etc. (see page 137).

Verbs in *-ciare* and *-giare* drop the *i* before *e* or *i*:

e.g. COMINCIARE *to begin*
io com*i*ncio

BUT tu cominci, noi cominceremo, *etc.*

VIAGGIARE *to travel*
io vi*a*ggio

BUT tu viaggi, noi viaggeremo, *etc.*

VOCABULARY

il vi*a*ggio	journey	cominciare	to begin
il passaporto	passport	dec*i*dere (*p.p.* deciso)	to decide
l'itiner*a*rio	itinerary		
il saluto	greeting	potere	to be able
la fine	end	volere	to want
*e*ssere occupato	to be busy	venire (*p.p.* venuto)	to come
in *o*rdine	in order		
ecco perchè	that is why	sapere (*irr.*)	to know; *so*, I know
l*i*bero	free		
ultimamente	lately, recently	contento	pleased
sinceramente	sincerely	occupato	occupied, busy
viaggiare	to travel	l'uff*i*cio	office
preparare	to prepare, get ready	domani	tomorrow
		se	if

UNA L*E*TTERA

Piazza Alberto, 43,
Londra.
4 aprile 1960.

Caro Signor M*a*rio,

Non ho potuto visitarLa ultimamente perchè sono stato molto occupato, ecco perchè Le scrivo questa l*e*ttera.

Quando avrà le vacanze? Le mie cominceranno alla fine di l*u*glio, avrò tre settimane quest'anno; e Lei, quante settimane avrà?

Ho deciso di fare un altro vi*a*ggio in It*a*lia ed ho già preparato un bell'itiner*a*rio. Potrà venire con me? So che ha sempre desiderato fare un secondo vi*a*ggio in It*a*lia.

È in *o*rdine il Suo passaporto? Io sarò in città questo s*a*bato, e se Lei sarà l*i*bero potremo parlare insieme delle nostre vacanze.

Uscirò dal mio uff*i*cio a mezzogiorno e un quarto.

Tanti saluti a Lei ed alla Sua fam*i*glia.

Sinceramente Suo,

Giovanni.

EXERCISES

A. Answer in Italian:

1. Chi ha scritto una l*e*ttera?
2. A chi è scritta?
3. Perchè Giovanni non ha potuto visitare il suo amico?
4. Quando avrà le vacanze Giovanni?
5. Quante settimane avrà?
6. Che cosa ha deciso di fare?
7. Che cosa ha preparato?
8. Quando sarà in città?
9. A che ora?
10. A chi manda i suoi saluti?

B. Complete with the future of the verb in brackets, then translate:

1. Noi (parlare) italiano.
2. Carlo (ric*e*vere) una cartolina.
3. Lei non (capire) questa l*e*ttera.
4. Roberto e M*a*rio (avere) una vacanza.
5. Io non (*e*ssere) a Londra domani.

C. Replace the dash by a subject pronoun and then translate:

1. —— venderò l'autom*o*bile.
2. —— compreremo una casa.
3. —— finirai la l*e*ttera domani.
4. —— sarete occupati.
5. —— potrà capire questa lezione.

D. Translate:

1. Mario and John will go to Italy.
2. They will travel together.
3. My holidays begin today.
4. I am going to London tomorrow.
5. John is able to speak Italian very well.
6. I can speak a little.
7. The passport is not in order.
8. We have decided to stay at home.
9. Do you want to read this letter?
10. No, thank you, I am too busy.

E. Give the first person singular of the perfect and future tenses of the following verbs:

1. preparare
2. cr*e*dere
3. finire
4. avere
5. *e*ssere
6. potere
7. viaggiare
8. andare
9. fare
10. dare

LESSON XV

Conditional Tense

The conditional tense, as already stated in the previous lesson, is formed from the infinitive less the final vowel. The following endings are then added to the infinitive:

First person singular	-ei
Second person singular	-esti
Third person singular	-ebbe
First person plural	-emmo
Second person plural	-este
Third person plural	-*e*bbero

Note the double *m* of the first person plural which distinguishes it from the first person plural of the future tense.

As in the future tense, the *a* of the infinitive of regular verbs in *-are* must be changed to *e*.

Now let us study the conditional tense of the three model verbs.

CONDITIONAL TENSE

PARLARE		V*E*NDERE	
parlerei	*I should* or *would speak*, etc.	venderei	*I should* or *would sell*, etc.
parleresti		venderesti	
parlerebbe		venderebbe	
parleremmo		venderemmo	
parlereste		vendereste	
parler*e*bbero		vender*e*bbero	

CAPIRE

capirei	*I should* or *would understand*, etc.
capiresti	
capirebbe	
capiremmo	
capireste	
capir*e*bbero	

The conditional of the auxiliaries *avere* and *essere* has the same stem as that of the future, *avr-* and *sar-*; and to these stems the endings of the conditional, which are the same for all verbs, are added:

AVERE		ESSERE	
avrei	*I should* or	sarei	*I should* or
avresti	*would have*,	saresti	*would be*, etc.
avrebbe	etc.	sarebbe	
avremmo		saremmo	
avreste		sareste	
avrebbero		sarebbero	

Some Geographical Terms

COUNTRIES		INHABITANTS	
L'Inghilterra	*England*	Gl'Inglesi	*English*
La Francia	*France*	I Francesi	*French*
L'Italia	*Italy*	Gl'Italiani	*Italians*
La Svizzera	*Switzerland*	Gli Svizzeri	*Swiss*
La Spagna	*Spain*	Gli Spagnoli	*Spaniards*
La Germania	*Germany*	I Tedeschi	*Germans*
Il Portogallo	*Portugal*	I Portoghesi	*Portuguese*
L'America	*America*	Gli Americani	*Americans*
La Russia	*Russia*	I Russi	*Russians*

CAPITALS

Londra	*London*	Madrid	*Madrid*
Parigi	*Paris*	Berlino	*Berlin*
Roma	*Rome*	Lisbona	*Lisbon*
Berna	*Berne*	Mosca	*Moscow*

NOTE.—All cities except *il Cairo* are feminine.

CARDINAL POINTS

Nouns:		Adjectives:	
il nord *or* settentrione	*North*	settentrionale	*northern*
il sud *or* mezzogiorno	*South*	meridionale	*southern*
l'est, il levante *or* l'oriente	*East*	orientale	*eastern*
		occidentale	*western*
l'ovest, il ponente *or* l'occidente	*West*	centrale	*central*

VOCABULARY

abitare	to live, dwell	la Banca Commerciale	Commercial Bank
la risposta	reply	*o*ttimo	excellent
la guida*	guide	v*a*lido	valid
una volta	once	distinti saluti	kind regards
il luogo	place	dunque	therefore, then
il paese	country	a s*a*bato!	till Saturday
il punto cardinale	cardinal point	pr*o*ssimo	next
la Riviera di Ponente	western Riviera	scorso	last
la Riviera di Levante	eastern Riviera	ancora	still, yet
aspettare	to wait for	G*e*nova	Genoa
la porta principale	main door	stamani *or* stamattina	this morning
		i genitori	parents
		i parenti	relations

*The noun *guida* is always feminine, even when referring to a man.

LA RISPOSTA

Via Trafalgar, 25,
Londra.
9 aprile 1960.

Caro Signor Giovanni,

Gr*a*zie della Sua l*e*ttera che ho ricevuta stamattina. Quest'anno anch'io avrò le vacanze alla fine di l*u*glio e sarò molto contento di venire con Lei in It*a*lia.

Lei ha visitato tante belle città e così sarebbe, per me, un'*o*ttima guida. Il mio passaporto è v*a*lido ancora per due anni.

È vero che sono stato una volta in It*a*lia, ma ho visitato soltanto la Riviera di Ponente ed alcuni bei luoghi fra Ventim*i*glia e G*e*nova; non sono stato ancora nelle altre città.

Sarò l*i*bero, anch'io, s*a*bato pr*o*ssimo, dopo mezzogiorno, e L'aspetterò davanti alla porta principale della Banca Commerciale. Potrebbe fare colazione con me? Così avremmo molto tempo per parlare delle vacanze estive. A s*a*bato dunque!

Distinti saluti ai Suoi genitori ed a Lei,

M*a*rio.

EXERCISES

A. Answer the following:

1. Chi ha ricevuto una l*e*ttera?
2. È stato in It*a*lia M*a*rio?
3. Chi sarebbe una buona guida per lui?
4. Quando sarà l*i*bero?
5. Dove aspetterà il suo amico?
6. Che potr*e*bbero fare tutti e due?
7. A chi manda dei saluti?
8. Qual è la capitale d'Inghilterra?
9. Dove abita il signor M*a*rio?
10. Dove abita Lei?

B. Translate:

1. The English speak English.
2. The French speak French.
3. The Italians speak Italian.
4. The Germans speak German.
5. The Spaniards speak Spanish.
6. Madrid is the capital of Spain.
7. Berne is the capital of Switzerland.
8. Paris is the capital of France.
9. Rome is the capital of Italy.
10. The four cardinal points are North, South, East, West.

C. (*a*) Translate:

il settentrione   il mezzogiorno   l'oriente
l'occidente   centrale

(*b*) Put into the plural:

un Tedesco   un Inglese
uno Spagnolo   uno Sv*i*zzero
un Francese   un Americano

D. Translate:

1. I have not received a letter today.
2. We would be pleased.
3. I would be able to come.
4. They would receive a postcard.

5. We send our greetings to all.
6. This Bank is very big.
7. That Bank is small.
8. I have only seen one newspaper today.
9. The western Riviera is very beautiful.
10. We will not visit the eastern Riviera this time.

E. Write the conditional of:

(*a*) cantare (*b*) ric*e*vere (*c*) finire
(*d*) avere (*e*) *e*ssere

SVIZZERA
AUSTRIA
UNGHERIA
FRANCIA
Trentino
Trento
Venezia-Giulia
Lombardia
Milano
Piemonte
Torino
Veneto
Trieste
Venezia
IUGO-SLAVIA
Emilia
Bologna
Liguria
Genova
Mare Adriatico
Mare Ligure
Firenze
Ancona
Toscana
Perugia
Marche
Umbria
L'Aquila
Lazio
ROMA
Abruzzi e Molise
Mare Tirreno
Sardegna
Cagliari
Bari
Campania
Napoli
Puglia
Potenza
Basili-cata
Calabria
Palermo
Reggio
Sicilia
Mare Ionio
Mare Mediterraneo
N
O
E
S

LESSON XVI

Irregular Plurals of Nouns

There are some nouns, mostly of Greek origin, which end in *-ca*, *-ta*, *-ma* or *-ga*, and which are masculine, forming their plural in *-i*:

e.g. il duca	*the duke*	→ i duchi
il poeta	*the poet*	→ i poeti
il poema	*the poem*	→ i poemi
il collega	*the colleague*	→ i colleghi
Note also: il Papa	*the Pope*	→ i Papi

There are nouns ending in *-ista* which are of both genders; these have a masculine plural in *-i* and a feminine plural in *-e*:

e.g. il pianista	*the pianist* (*m.*)	→ i pianisti
la pianista	*the pianist* (*f.*)	→ le pianiste
un artista	*an artist* (*m.*)	→ degli artisti
un'artista	*an artist* (*f.*)	→ delle artiste

The 18 Regions of Italy

Italy is divided into 18 regions, each of which has its chief town.

Le Regioni, *the regions*		I Capoluoghi, *the chief towns*	
L'Italia settentrionale, *Northern Italy*			
1. Il Piemonte	*Piedmont*	Torino	*Turin*
2. La Liguria	*Liguria*	Genova	*Genoa*
3. La Lombardia	*Lombardy*	Milano	*Milan*
4. L'Emilia	*Emilia*	Bologna	*Bologna*
5. Il Trentino *or* Venezia Tridentina	*Trentino*	Trento	*Trent*
6. Il Veneto *or* Venezia Euganea	*Venetia*	Venezia	*Venice*
7. La Venezia Giulia	*Venezia Giulia*	Trieste	*Trieste*

L'It*a*lia centrale, *Central Italy*

8. La Toscana	*Tuscany*	Firenze	*Florence*
9. Le Marche	*The Marches*	Ancona	*Ancona*
10. L'*U*mbria	*Umbria*	Per*u*gia	*Perugia*
11. Il L*a*zio	*Latium*	Roma	*Rome*
12. Gli Abruzzi e Molise	*Abruzzi*	L'*A*quila	*Aquila*

L'It*a*lia meridionale, *Southern Italy*

13. La Camp*a*nia	*Campagna*	N*a*poli	*Naples*
14. La Basilicata *or* Luc*a*nia	*Basilicata*	Potenza	*Potenza*
15. La P*u*glia *or* Le P*u*glie	*Apulia*	Bari	*Bari*
16. La Cal*a*bria	*Calabria*	Reggio Cal*a*bria	*Reggio Calabria*

L'It*a*lia insulare, *Islands of Italy*

17. La Sic*i*lia	*Sicily*	Palermo	*Palermo*
18. La Sardegna	*Sardinia*	C*a*gliari	*Cagliari*

Note also the following:

Il Mare Mediterr*a*neo	*Mediterranean Sea*
Il Mare L*i*gure	*Ligurian Sea*
Il Mare Tirreno	*Tyrrhenian Sea*
Il Mare I*o*nio	*Ionian Sea*
Il Mare Adri*a*tico	*Adriatic Sea*

VOCABULARY

la carta geogr*a*fica	map	prima di	before
l'*i*sola	island	piacere	to please
la pen*i*sola	peninsula	mi piace	I like
la catena	chain	separare	to separate
le Alpi	Alps, high mountains	circondare	to surround
gli Appennini	Apennines	diverso	different
la spina dorsale	backbone	la preparazione	preparation
la regione	region	formare	to form
il capoluogo	chief town	l'*A*ustria	Austria
		la Iugosl*a*via	Jugoslavia
		cioè	that is, namely

PREPARARSI PER IL VI*A*GGIO

Prima di fare il loro vi*a*ggio Giovanni e M*a*rio gu*a*rdano una carta geogr*a*fica d'It*a*lia. V*e*dono la grande pen*i*sola con la catena delle Alpi a Nord. Le Alpi sep*a*rano l'It*a*lia dalla Fr*a*ncia, dalla Sv*i*zzera, dall'*A*ustria e dalla Iugosl*a*via. Gli Appennini f*o*rmano una spina dorsale all'It*a*lia. Il Mare Mediterr*a*neo circonda la pen*i*sola. Questo mare prende diversi nomi, cioè—
Mare L*i*gure, Mare Tirreno ad Ovest, Mare I*o*nio a Sud, Mare Adri*a*tico ad Est.

Poi tutti e due st*u*diano le diciotto regioni ed i capoluoghi.

EXERCISES

A. Translate and answer the following:

1. Che gu*a*rdano Giovanni e M*a*rio prima di fare il loro vi*a*ggio?
2. Che v*e*dono a Nord della carta geogr*a*fica?
3. Quali montagne sep*a*rano l'It*a*lia dalla Fr*a*ncia?
4. Che f*o*rmano gli Appennini all'It*a*lia?
5. Quale mare circonda la pen*i*sola?
6. Mi dica i nomi dei mari.
7. Mi dica i nomi di due *i*sole.
8. Qual è il capoluogo del L*a*zio?
9. Qual è il capoluogo della Toscana?
10. Qual è il capoluogo dell'Em*i*lia?

B. Put into the plural:

1. Il poeta
2. Un telegramma
3. Quella pianista
4. Quel violinista
5. Il programma
6. Il duca
7. L'artista (*f.*)
8. Questo poema
9. Quel pilota
10. Questo diagramma

C. Translate:

1. We are looking at a map.
2. I have visited these towns.
3. Here is a programme.
4. There is a telegram for you.

5. I like this pianist (*m*.).
6. There are some beautiful poems in this book.
7. Is there a poet in this town?
8. The chief town of Lombardy is Milan.
9. The chief town of Liguria is Genoa.
10. The chief town of Umbria is Perugia.

D. Put into the conditional:

1. Parlerò con lui.
2. Avrà una vacanza.
3. Saranno felici.
4. Venderai la casa?
5. Darò loro questo programma.
6. Non andrete a Londra?
7. Faremo una gita intorno al lago.
8. Saranno a casa?
9. Finirò il lavoro.
10. Riceveremo quella l*e*ttera domani.

E. Translate the reading passage.

F. Write in full the conditional of:

(*a*) avere (*b*) *e*ssere
(*c*) cominciare (*d*) viaggiare

LESSON XVII

Nouns in *-cia* and *-gia*

To form the plural of nouns ending in *-cia* and *-gia* the general rules are:

(*a*) If the *i* is unstressed it is omitted in the plural, provided that *c* and *g* are preceded by a consonant or doubled:

e.g.	la m*a*ncia	*the tip*	→ le mance
	la f*a*ccia	*the face*	→ le facce
	la l*o*ggia	*the balcony*	→ le logge

(*b*) If the *i* is unstressed and *c* and *g* are preceded by a vowel, the plural is in *-cie* and *-gie*:

e.g.	la cam*i*cia	*the shirt*	→ le cam*i*cie
	la val*i*gia	*the suitcase*	→ le val*i*gie

(*c*) If the *i* is stressed, it is retained in the plural:

e.g.	la farmac*i*a	*the chemist*	→ le farmac*i*e
	la bug*i*a	*the lie, falsehood*	→ le bug*i*e

Irregular Verbs—*dovere, salire, uscire, scendere*

dovere	*to have to, to owe, to be obliged*
salire	*to ascend, go up*
uscire	*to go out*
sc*e*ndere	*to descend* is regular in the present indicative.

PRESENT INDICATIVE

DOVERE *p.p.* dovuto		SALIRE *p.p.* salito
devo *or* debbo	*I must, I have to,* etc.	salgo *I go up*, etc.
devi		sali
deve		sale
dobbiamo		saliamo
dovete		salite
d*e*vono *or* d*e*bbono		s*a*lgono

USCIRE *p.p.* uscito		SCENDERE *p.p.* sceso	
esco	*I go out*, etc.	scendo	*I descend*, etc.
esci		scendi	
esce		scende	
usciamo		scendiamo	
uscite		scendete	
*e*scono		sc*e*ndono	

NOTE.—*salire*, *scendere* and *uscire* are conjugated with *e*s*sere* in the compound tenses.

VOCABULARY

la partenza	departure	andare avanti	to go forward *or* in front
il biglietto	ticket		
il tassì (*or* taxi)	taxi	m*e*ttere (*p.p.* messo)	to put
l'autista (*m.*)	chauffeur		
la stazione	station	non . . . (*verb*) . . . che	only, but
il facchino	porter		
la m*a*ncia	tip	Le piace?	do you like?
la rete	luggage rack	mi piace	I like
la val*i*gia	suitcase	non mi piace	I do not like
il viaggiatore	passenger, traveller	la fr*e*ccia	arrow
		la cili*e*gia	cherry
seconda classe	second class	la prov*i*ncia	province
il posto riservato	reserved seat	la d*o*ccia	shower-bath
		l'ar*a*ncia	orange
il n*u*mero	number	*e*ssere di	to belong to
buon vi*a*ggio!	pleasant journey!	cortese	courteous, polite
seguire	to follow, continue	tardi	late

LA PARTENZA

Giovanni e M*a*rio sono pronti a partire, ora asp*e*ttano il tassì.

Mario. Il campanello suona.

Giovanni. Sarà l'autista. (*Prendono le valigie e salgono sul tassì.*)

Mario. (*All'autista.*) Alla stazione Victoria.

Giovanni. In meno di dieci minuti ci saremo; dobbiamo preparare i passaporti ed i biglietti.

Mario. A che ora parte il treno?
Giovanni. Alle tredici e trenta.
Mario. C'è ancora tempo, non sono che le tredici e cinque ed ecco la stazione!
(*Giovanni paga l'autista e un facchino prende le valigie.*)
Giovanni. (*Al facchino.*) Il treno per Folkestone.
Il Facchino. Hanno posti riservati?
Giovanni. Sì, di seconda classe, ecco i numeri, 32 e 34. (*Il facchino va avanti, sale sul treno e trova i loro posti. Giovanni e Mario devono mostrare i passaporti ed i biglietti e poi seguono il facchino.*)
Il Facchino. Ecco i Loro posti, signori; ho messo le valigie sulla rete.
Giovanni. Grazie. (*Gli dà una mancia.*)
Il Facchino. Grazie—e buon viaggio!
(*Dieci minuti più tardi il treno parte.*)

(*Segue*)

EXERCISES

A. Answer in Italian:

1. Dove vanno Giovanni e Mario quando il tassì arriva?
2. Chi prende le loro valigie alla stazione?
3. Dove mette le valigie il facchino?
4. Sono riservati i loro posti sul treno?
5. Che cosa danno Giovanni e Mario al facchino?
6. A che ora parte il treno per Folkestone?
7. Viaggiano in prima classe Giovanni e Mario?
8. Che dice il facchino ai nostri viaggiatori?
9. Le piace viaggiare, signore?
10. Fa (Lei) un viaggio tutti gli anni?

B. Give the first person singular and plural of the following verbs in the future and the conditional:

1. dare
2. andare
3. preparare
4. prendere
5. partire
6. salire
7. uscire
8. dire
9. seguire
10. viaggiare

C. Give the opposites of the following verbs:

(*a*)
1. andare
2. arrivare
3. comprare
4. entrare
5. salire

(*b*) Put into the plural:
1. la fr*e*ccia
2. la cili*e*gia
3. la prov*i*ncia
4. l'ar*a*ncia
5. la farmacia

D. Translate:

1. I am waiting for my friend.
2. Where is the taxi?
3. Here it is.
4. I must prepare my suitcase.
5. My passport is in order.
6. Here are the tickets.
7. It is nearly midday.
8. The train leaves at 1.0 p.m.
9. This porter is very polite.
10. The train for Folkestone has left.

E. Translate:

1. Vado a comprare delle arance.
2. Questa val*i*gia è del signor Monti.
3. I viaggiatori danno delle mance ai facchini.
4. Dobbiamo seguire questo facchino.
5. Io andrò avanti.
6. Non mi piace questo posto.
7. Qual è il nostro treno?
8. Sarà quello.
9. Questo facchino riceverà una buona m*a*ncia.
10. Ecco il suo passaporto, dov'è il mio?

LESSON XVIII

Orthographic Changes in certain Verbs

As already stated, verbs ending in *-ciare* and *-giare* drop the *i* before another *e* or *i*: but all other verbs ending in *-iare* drop the *i* only before another *i*:

e.g. studiare	*to study*	(io)	st*u*dio
		(tu)	studi
		(noi)	studiamo

BUT studieremo, *we shall study*

Verbs ending in *-care* and *-gare* take an *h* between

c and *e*	*g* and *e*
c and *i*	*g* and *i*

to retain the hard sound of the infinitive. *Cercare* (to look for) and *pagare* (to pay, pay for) are typical examples.

PRESENT INDICATIVE

CERCARE		PAGARE	
(io) cerco	*I am looking for*, etc.	(io) pago	*I pay*, etc.
cerchi		paghi	
cerca		paga	
cerchiamo		paghiamo	
cercate		pagate	
cercano		p*a*gano	

Whereas in the present indicative the *h* appears only in the second person singular and the first person plural, it appears in all the persons of the future and conditional:

cercherò, *etc.*	*and* cercherei, *etc.*
pagherò, *etc.*	*and* pagherei, *etc.*

This orthographic change only occurs in verbs of the first conjugation: compare the verb *leggere*, to read:

leggo, leggi, legge, *etc.*

There is one important rule to note regarding verbs ending in *-cere*—an *i* is inserted before the *u* of the past participle:

e.g. conoscere	*to know*	*p.p.* conosciuto
piacere	*to please*	*p.p.* piaciuto

Negative Expressions

non	....	niente	*nothing*
or non	....	nulla	
non	....	mai	*never*
non	....	più	*no more, no longer*
non	....	nessuno	*nobody, no one*
non	....	che	*only, but*
non	....	nè . . . nè	*neither . . . nor*
non	....	mica	*not, not at all*

In an Italian sentence two negatives are often used together but they convey a single negative idea, not an affirmative as in English.

e.g. Margherita non capisce niente.
Margaret does not understand anything.
Carlo non ha mai veduto questo città.
Charles has never seen this town.
Caterina non ha nè fratello nè sorella.
Catherine has neither brother nor sister.

Sometimes these negative expressions are used without *non* but in this case they must precede the verb:

e.g. Mai scrivo. *I never write* (= non scrivo mai).
Nulla vediamo. *We see nothing* (= non vediamo nulla).
Nessuno viene. *No one comes.*

VOCABULARY

il giornale	newspaper	il controllo	control
la rivista	magazine	la M*a*nica	Straits of Dover, English Channel
la costa	coast		
la v*i*sita	visit	il segno	sign
ia dogana	customs	il pezzo	piece
l doganiere	customs officer	il gesso	chalk

il piroscafo	steamer	prendere, *p.p.* preso	to take
far domande	to ask questions	lasciare	to leave
allora	then	cercare	to look for
soltanto, solo, solamente	only	pagare	to pay for
		richiedere	to require
scendere, *p.p.* sceso	to descend, go down	il finestrino	carriage window
		fra	in, within

DA LONDRA A FOLKESTONE

Giovanni. Ora cominciamo il nostro viaggio. Ha portato dei giornali, non è vero?

Mario. Sì, eccoli! Ho portato anche delle riviste, eccole.

Giovanni. Grazie.

Mario. Prego; fra due ore saremo a Folkestone, non è vero?

Giovanni. Sè, e poi ci sarà la visita alla dogana.

Mario. E dovremo aprire le valigie?

Giovanni. Non sempre, fanno soltanto domande, ma c'è il controllo dei passaporti che richiede molto tempo. (*Tutti e due leggono i giornali.*)

Mario (*che guarda dal finestrino*). Io vedo la Manica.

Giovanni. Siamo quasi arrivati allora, come passa il tempo! (*Il treno si ferma, i nostri viaggiatori si preparano, scendono dal treno e vanno alla dogana. La visita non richiede tanto tempo; il doganiere fa un segno misterioso su ogni valigia, con un pezzo di gesso, e poi Giovanni e Mario salgono sul piroscafo.*)

Mario. Presto lasceremo la costa inglese e fra un'ora vedremo la costa francese.

(*Segue*)

EXERCISES

A. Answer the following:

1. Chi ha portato dei giornali?
2. Quando arriveranno a Folkestone i viaggiatori?
3. Dobbiamo aprire sempre le valigie alla dogana?
4. Che vede, Mario, dal finestrino?
5. Che fanno i viaggiatori?

6. Dove vanno poi?
7. Richiede poco tempo la *v*isita alla dogana?
8. Che fanno i doganieri su ogni val*i*gia?
9. E poi dove s*a*lgono i viaggiatori?
10. Quando vedranno la costa francese?

B. Give the first persons singular and plural of the following verbs in the present indicative:

1. cercare
2. fare
3. salire
4. pagare
5. andare

C. Translate:

1. I will read this newspaper.
2. What are you reading, John?
3. I am reading an Italian magazine.
4. At what time will this train arrive at Folkestone?
5. In an hour, sir.
6. We have almost arrived.
7. The train is stopping.
8. I can only find one magazine.
9. Here is the other one.
10. There is nothing in this box.

D. Translate:

1. Dove sono andati i facchini?
2. Mi piace il mare quando è calmo.
3. Io preferisco il mare grosso.
4. Eccoli, s*a*lgono sul pir*o*scafo.
5. Questo pir*o*scafo non è grande.
6. Partiremo alle qu*i*ndici.
7. A che ora arriveremo a Folkestone?
8. Verso le qu*i*ndici e venti.
9. Ecco la mia val*i*gia, dov'è la sua?
10. *E*ccola, vicino al facchino.

E. Conjugate, in the interrogative form, the future of:

(*a*) arrivare (*b*) cercare

LESSON XIX

More Nouns with Irregular Plurals

Nouns of one syllable, those ending in an accented vowel, and a few ending in a consonant (usually of foreign origin) have no distinctive change of termination in the plural:

e.g. il re	*king*	→ i re
il dì	*day (poet.)*	→ i dì
la città	*town*	→ le città
il lapis	*pencil*	→ i lapis
l'autob*us*	*motor bus*	→ gli autob*us*
il bar	*bar*	→ i bar
il caffè	*café, coffee*	→ i caffè

Note also:

la frutta	*fruit*	→ le frutta
l'uovo	*egg*	→ le uova
il lenzuolo	*sheet*	→ le lenzuola
un centin*a*io	*about a hundred*	→ centin*a*ia, *hundreds*
un migli*a*io	*about a thousand*	→ migli*a*ia, *thousands*
il dito	*finger*	→ le dita
il br*a*ccio	*arm*	→ le br*a*ccia
la m*o*glie	*wife*	→ le m*o*gli
il muro	*wall (of city)*	→ le mura
BUT l'uomo	*man*	→ gli u*o*mini

Irregular Verbs—*bere, sapere, conoscere*

BERE (*contracted from* bevere), *to drink*
The present tense is quite regular:

bevo	*I am drinking*, etc.
bevi	
beve	
beviamo	
bevete	
b*e*vono	

But note the stem of the future which is irregular:

berrò *I shall drink*, etc.
berrai
berrà
berremo
berrete
berranno

The conditional endings are added to the stem of the future:

berrei, berresti, *etc.*

SAPERE *to know a fact* *p.p.* saputo
CONOSCERE *to be acquainted with people, places*, etc. *p.p.* conosciuto

PRESENT INDICATIVE

so	conosco
sai	conosci
sa	conosce
sappiamo	conosciamo
sapete	conoscete
sanno	conoscono

Note that *sapere* can also mean "to know how to", as in the following example with *spiegarsi*:

so spiegarmi *I know how to explain myself*, etc.
sai spiegarti
sa spiegarsi
sappiamo spiegarci
sapete spiegarvi
sanno spiegarsi

Similarly,
so nuotare *I know how to swim*

VOCABULARY

la traversata	crossing	fare la fila	to form a queue
il bar	bar	il ponte, la coperta	deck
la sigaretta	cigarette	a bordo	on board
il fiammifero	match	la macchina fotografica	camera
il cerino	wax match		
la fila	queue, line		

fare una fotografia	to take a photograph	s*u*bito	at once
vis*i*bile	visible	dimenticare	to forget
sembrare	to seem	andiamo	let us go
bere	to drink	pesante	heavy
costare	to cost	leggero	light
evitare	to avoid	la fame	hunger
rallentare	to slow down	aver fame	to be hungry
sbarcare	to disembark	la sete	thirst
		aver sete	to be thirsty

LA TRAVERSATA DELLA M*A*NICA

Giovanni. Come è calma la M*a*nica oggi. Sembra un lago!

Mario. Quanti viaggiatori! Dove vanno tutti?

Giovanni. Alcuni andranno in Fr*a*ncia, altri in Sv*i*zzera o in It*a*lia.

Mario. Quanto dura questa traversata?

Giovanni. Un'ora e venticinque minuti. Des*i*dera bere qualche cosa?

Mario. Sì, andiamo al bar. Allo stesso tempo potremo comprare sigarette e cerini: le sigarette c*o*stano meno sul pir*o*scafo.

Giovanni. Non dimentichiamo che ci sarà un altro controllo di passaporti prima di arrivare a Calais, fatto a bordo.

Mario. Possiamo andare s*u*bito all'uff*i*cio.

Giovanni. È una buon'idea! Così eviteremo di fare la fila.

Mario. Dov'è la mia m*a*cchina fotogr*a*fica? Vorrei fare alcune fotografie prima di sbarcare. Vedo facchini francesi che si prep*a*rano a venire a bordo.

Giovanni. Il pir*o*scafo rallenta, dobbiamo prepararci anche noi. (*A Calais i facchini salgono sul piroscafo per aiutare i viaggiatori con le loro valigie. Dopo una visita alla dogana francese i viaggiatori salgono sul treno continentale.*)

(*Segue*)

EXERCISES

A. Answer the following:

1. È sempre agitato il mare?
2. Quali paesi visiteranno i viaggiatori?

3. Chi des*i*dera bere qualche cosa?
4. Dove vanno Giovanni e M*a*rio?
5. Che c*o*mprano al bar?
6. Perchè c*o*mprano sigarette?
7. Dove ci sarà un controllo di passaporti?
8. Per evitare di fare la fila, che faranno Giovanni e M*a*rio?
9. Che vorrebbe fare M*a*rio prima di sbarcare?
10. Che fanno i facchini francesi?

B. Give the third persons singular and plural of the following verbs in the future tense:

1. evitare
2. spiegare
3. stare
4. bere
5. andare

C. Put into the plural:

1. Quel re
2. Quella città
3. Quell'uomo
4. Un uovo
5. L'amico francese
6. L'amica inglese
7. Una rivista tedesca
8. Un viaggiatore sv*i*zzero
9. Una m*a*cchina fotogr*a*fica
10. Un artista italiano

D. Translate:

1. Do you want any cigarettes?
2. Yes, and some matches too.
3. How much do they cost?
4. I do not know, we shall ask the price.
5. Do you know that lady?
6. Yes, I met her in London.
7. These suitcases are not heavy.
8. Mine is very light.
9. This pianist (*f.*) plays well.
10. This town is very modern.
11. Are you hungry, John?
12. No, but I am thirsty.

E. Conjugate in the conditional:

(*a*) sbarcare (*b*) fare

LESSON XX

Adverbs

We have already met several adverbs in the previous lessons:

e.g. molto	*very; very much*	sempre	*always*
poco	*little*	oggi	*today*
bene	*well*	di solito	*usually*
quasi	*almost*	sì	*yes*
dove	*where*	no	*no*
davanti	*in front*	non	*not*

As a rule the adverb is placed immediately after the verb, except *non* which always precedes the verb.

The adverb "only" may be rendered by *non* in front of the verb and *che* after it, or by *solo, soltanto* or *solamente*:

e.g. Non ho che
Ho solo
Ho soltanto
Ho solamente } due fratelli. *I have only two brothers.*

The adverb "ago" is rendered by *fa.*

Formation of Adverbs

Adverbs of manner are usually formed by adding *-mente* to the feminine singular of the adjective:

e.g. caro, cara → caramente *dearly*
felice → felicemente *happily*

If, however, the adjective ends in *-le* or *-re*, the final vowel is dropped before *-mente* is added:

e.g. facile → facilmente *easily*
particolare → particolarmente *particularly*

unless there are two consonants preceding the vowel, in which case *-mente* is added to the adjective itself:

e.g. folle → follemente *madly*

Impersonal Verbs

True impersonal verbs are used only in the third person singular. Many of these verbs pertain to the weather.

e.g. piovere	*to rain;*	piove	*it is raining*
tonare *or* tuonare	*to thunder;*	tuona	*it is thundering*
lampeggiare	*to lighten;*	lampeggia	*it lightens, there is lightning*
gelare	*to freeze;*	gela	*it is freezing*

They are usually conjugated with the auxiliary *essere* in the compound tenses (*piovere* may take *avere* or *essere*):

e.g. è (ha) piovuto *it rained* è gelato *it froze*

Besides these true impersonal verbs, there are also impersonal expressions formed with certain verbs:

e.g. FARE	fa caldo	*it is warm*	ha fatto caldo, *it was warm*, etc.
	fa freddo	*it is cold*	
	fa bel tempo	*it is fine* (*weather*)	
TIRARE	tira vento	*it is windy*	ha tirato vento, *it was windy*
ANDARE	va bene	*it is all right*	
STARE	sta bene		

NOTE.—*Fare* and *tirare* are conjugated with *avere* in the compound tenses.

Of other impersonal verbs the most common are:

BISOGNARE	*to be necessary*
bisogna	*it is necessary*
BASTARE	*to be enough, to suffice*
basta	*it is enough*
SEMBRARE *or* PARERE	*to seem, to appear*
sembra *or* pare	*it seems*
PIACERE	*to please*
piace	*it pleases*; piacciono (*pl.*), *they please*

A sentence such as "I like this flower" is translated *Mi piace questo fiore*, lit. "This flower pleases me".

BUT "I like these flowers" must be translated *Mi piacciono questi fiori*, lit. "These flowers please me".

NOTE.—The use of the impersonal verb with all the conjunctive pronouns:

mi piace	questa casa	*I like*	*this house*
ti piace		*you like*	
gli piace		*he likes*	
le piace		*she likes*	
Le piace		*you like*	
ci piace		*we like*	
vi piace		*you like*	
piace loro		*they like*	
piace Loro		*you like*	
mi pi*a*cciono	queste case	*I like*	*these houses*
ti pi*a*cciono		*you like*	
etc.		etc.	

NOTE.—Non mi piace (pi*a*cciono) . . . , *I do not like* . . .
BUT mi dispiace, *I am sorry*, lit. *it displeases me*.

The impersonal verb SEMBRARE, *to seem*, with the conjunctive pronouns.

mi sembra	*It seems to*	*me*
ti sembra		*you*
gli sembra		*him*
le sembra		*her*
Le sembra		*you*
ci sembra		*us*
vi sembra		*you*
sembra loro		*them*
sembra Loro		*you*

The plural form is:

mi sembrano *they seem to me*, etc.

The impersonal verb TOCCARE, *to be the turn of*, used with the expression, A chi tocca? *Whose turn is it?*

Note the disjunctive pronouns.

tocca a me		*my turn*
tocca a te		*your turn*
tocca a lui		*his turn*
tocca a lei		*her turn*
tocca a Lei	*it is*	*your turn*
tocca a noi		*our turn*
tocca a voi		*your turn*
tocca a loro		*their turn*
tocca a Loro		*your turn*

VOCABULARY

il risotto	savoury rice dish	bastare	to be enough
gli gnocchi	very small dumplings	piacere	to please
la bistecca	steak	scommettere	to bet
l'abbacchio	young roast lamb	alla	in the manner of
l'agnello	lamb	Chianti	red or white wine of Chianti, a district in Tuscany
il rosmarino	rosemary	Valpolicella	a noted red wine of the province of Verona
basta!	that is enough! that will do!	Moscato	wine made from muscatel grapes
semplicemente	simply	Orvieto	the white wine of Orvieto, town in Umbria
spumante	sparkling	Asti Spumante	sparkling wine of Asti, town near Turin; Italian champagne
noto	noted	Montefiascone	a town near Rome
tenero	tender	la sciampagna *or* lo "champagne"	champagne
timido	timid, shy	due giorni fa	two days ago
regolare	regular		
costare	to cost		
assaggiare	to taste		
arrostire	to roast		
arrosto	roast (*meat*)		
dolce	sweet		
costoso	expensive		
secco	dry		
scelto	choice (*adj.*)		
provare	to try		
consistere	to consist		

SUL TRENO CONTINENTALE

Giovanni. *E*ccoci finalmente sul treno continentale. Domani saremo in It*a*lia.

Mario. Quando sarò in It*a*lia vorrò provare molti piatti italiani; sa il nome di qualcuno?

Giovanni. Certo, per es*e*mpio
Risotto alla milanese
Gnocchi alla genovese
Bistecca alla fiorentina
Abb*a*cchio alla romana.

Mario. Ho già assaggiato i primi tre piatti, ma che cosa è l'abb*a*cchio alla romana?

Giovanni. È l'agnello arrosto con rosmarino; è buon*i*ssimo ed è molto t*e*nero.

Mario. Saprà anche i nomi di vini scelti, scommetto!

Giovanni. *E*ccone alcuni, Chianti, Valpolicella, Moscato, Orvieto ed il famoso Est! Est! Est! e poi non dimentichiamo l'Asti Spumante, lo "champagne" italiano.

Mario. Mi dica, per favore, che cosa è Est! Est! Est!

Giovanni. Un vino noto, di Montefiascone; è buono ma forte.

Mario. Basta! Mi fa venire sete.

(*Segue*)

EXERCISES

A. Answer the following:

1. Che farà Mario quando arriverà in It*a*lia?
2. Le piace il risotto alla milanese, signore?
3. Le pi*a*cciono gli gnocchi alla genovese?
4. Che cosa è l'abb*a*cchio alla romana?
5. Preferisce il vino rosso o il vino bianco?
6. È sempre t*e*nera la carne?
7. Conosce (Lei) molte città italiane?
8. Sa Lei che ora è adesso?
9. A che ora parte (Lei) da casa la mattina?
10. A che ora arriva in uff*i*cio?
11. Le piace viaggiare in treno?
12. Preferisce viaggiare in m*a*cchina?

B. Form adverbs from the following adjectives:

1. fortunato
2. diff*i*cile
3. t*i*mido
4. regolare
5. folle

C. Translate:

1. I like this view.
2. I do not like these postcards.
3. Do you like these colours?
4. I prefer this colour to that one.
5. This wine is very good.
6. How much does it cost?
7. It is not very expensive.
8. Do you prefer a sweet wine?
9. I like Asti Spumante very much.
10. I like nearly all wines.

D. Put into the plural:

1. Un vino secco.
2. Una bistecca t*e*nera.
3. Questo vino è buono.
4. Quella sigaretta mi piace.
5. Questa veduta mi sembra bella.

E. (*a*) Translate:

1. It seems to him.
2. It seems to us.
3. Does it seem to them?
4. Is this enough?
5. These are not enough.

(*b*) Conjugate in the negative form the conditional of *sapere*.

REVISION TEST

A. Give the past participle of:

1. amare	6. servire
2. fare	7. pr*e*ndere
3. bere	8. *e*ssere
4. l*e*ggere	9. dire
5. scr*i*vere	10. aprire.

B. Change the verbs in the following sentences to the present perfect, and translate:

1. Questo studente lavora bene.
2. Maria e Caterina scr*i*vono male.
3. Roberto è in campagna.
4. I ragazzi p*a*rtono oggi.
5. Carlo cerca il suo cane.

C. Translate the word in brackets:

1. Giuseppe non dice (*anything*).
2. Una settimana (*ago*)
3. La casa è (*in front of*) il lago.
4. (*There is*) una chiesa (*near to*) la scuola.
5. (*That*) *a*lbero è magn*i*fico.

D. Translate:

1. I have only one brother.
2. Margaret has neither uncle nor aunt.
3. We have nothing in this basket.
4. Paul no longer studies English.
5. We have never seen these lakes.

E. Put into the plural:

1. il violinista	6. l'autob*u*s
2. la pianista	7. il re
3. l'uovo	8. la mia mano
4. quell'uomo	9. il br*a*ccio
5. quella città	10. questa frutta

F. Give the opposites:

1. rispondere
2. partire
3. uscire
4. salire
5. andare
6. la settimana scorsa
7. il primo giorno
8. davanti a
9. sopra la *ta*vola
10. lontano dalla stazione

G. Insert an object pronoun and translate:

1. —— vedo.
2. —— prendiamo.
3. —— avrà.
4. —— faremo.
5. —— parlo.
6. —— piace.
7. —— farà.
8. —— sembra.
9. —— comprerebbe.
10. —— b*a*stano.

H. Translate:

1. This telegram is for her.
2. These letters are for me.
3. That postcard will be from him.
4. Margaret has been with us.
5. Paul will not go with you (2nd per. sing.).

I. (*a*) Form adverbs from the following adjectives:

1. sincero
2. *u*tile
3. triste
4. generoso
5. particolare

(*b*) Conjugate the following:

Non sarò a casa domani.
Vorrei una vacanza.

J. (*a*) Write the perfect tense of *divertirsi*.

(*b*) Write the future tense of *alzarsi*.

SECTION THREE

LESSON XXI

The Gerund

The gerund corresponds to the English present participle and it is invariable. To form the gerund:

-ando is added to the stem of verbs ending in *-are*
-endo is added to the stem of verbs ending in *-ere* and *-ire*

e.g. parlare	parlando	*speaking*
v*e*ndere	vendendo	*selling*
capire	capendo	*understanding*

The Italian gerund is not governed by a preposition or a conjunction:

e.g. "When buying" is translated by *comprando* alone.
"While reading" is translated by *leggendo* alone.
"On saying" is translated by *dicendo* alone.

Note, however, that the endings *-ando* and *-endo* are added to the original stem of verbs which have a contracted form:

e.g. dire (contracted from d*i*cere), dicendo
fare (contracted from f*a*cere), facendo
bere (contracted from b*e*vere), bevendo

The Progressive Construction

The gerund is sometimes used with the verbs *stare* and *andare* (*stare* being more commonly used), forming a progressive construction and implying more emphasis:

e.g. sto leggendo	*I am reading*
stiamo parlando	*we are speaking*

Besides the gerund some Italian verbs have a present participle ending in *-ante*, pl. *-anti*, and *-ente*, pl. *-enti* which is either a noun or an adjective:

e.g. un insegnante	*a teacher*
la Torre Pendente	*the Leaning Tower*

Irregular Verbs—*mettere, chiudere, venire*

Many irregular verbs are irregular only in the past participle and the past definite (see Lesson XXIV).

m*e*ttere	*to put*	*p.p.* messo
chi*u*dere	*to close*	*p.p.* chiuso
venire	*to come*	*p.p.* venuto

The present, the future and the conditional of many irregular verbs are regularly formed.

PRESENT	FUTURE	CONDITIONAL
metto, *etc.*	metterò, *etc.*	metterei, *etc.*
chiudo, *etc.*	chiuderò, *etc.*	chiuderei, *etc.*

Note the irregular forms of VENIRE, to come.

PRESENT		FUTURE		CONDITIONAL	
vengo	*I come, am*	verrò	*I shall*	verrei	*I would*
vieni	*coming*, etc.	verrai	*come*, etc.		*come*, etc.
viene		verrà			
veniamo		verremo			
venite		verrete			
v*e*ngono		verranno			

NOTE.—*Mettere* and *chiudere* are conjugated with *avere* in the compound tenses, but *venire* is conjugated with *e*ss*ere*.

m*e*ttere	ho messo	*I put*, etc.
chi*u*dere	ho chiuso	*I closed*, etc.
BUT venire	sono venuto(a)	*I came*, etc.

The Human Body—*il corpo umano*

la testa *or* il capo	*head*
il capello, i capelli	*hair*
la fronte	*forehead*
l'*o*cchio, gli occhi	*eye*(*s*)
il naso	*nose*
la gu*a*ncia, le guance	*cheek*(*s*)
la bocca, le bocche	*mouth*(*s*)
il dente	*tooth*
il labbro, le labbra	*lip*(*s*)

il mento	*chin*
l'orecchio, le orecchie	*ear(s)*
il ginocchio, le ginocchia	*knee(s)*
il membro, le membra	*limb(s)*
il collo	*neck*
la gola	*throat*
la spalla	*shoulder*
il braccio, le braccia	*arm(s)*
la mano, le mani	*hand(s)*
il dito, le dita	*finger(s)*
la gamba	*leg*
il piede	*foot*
il cuore	*heart*

As seen from this vocabulary, certain nouns, mostly pertaining to the human body, are *masculine* in the singular and *feminine* in the plural.

Note the following expressions with *avere*:

aver mal di testa *or* mal di capo	*to have*	*a headache*
aver mal di denti		*a toothache*
aver mal di gola		*a sore throat*
aver male a un dito		*a sore finger*
aver male agli occhi		*sore eyes* or *eye trouble*

VOCABULARY

il vagone ristorante	Restaurant Car	a causa di	on account of
		seguente	following
lo sportello	carriage door	di solito	usually
il paesaggio	scenery	di nuovo	again
la *Superba*	The "Mighty", "Superb"	montagnoso	mountainous
		collinoso	hilly
la ricchezza	wealth	commerciale	commercial
un palazzo	palace, large building	importante	important
		l'organo	organ
il corridoio	corridor	vitale	chief, vital
il porto	port	udire	to hear
la nave	ship	stare per	to be about to
la vista	view, sight	bellissimo	very beautiful
fino a	as far as	dormire	to sleep

L'ARRIVO IN IT*A*LIA

Mario (*la mattina seguente*). Buon giorno Giovanni, ha dormito bene?

Giovanni. Sì, ben*i*ssimo, di s*o*lito non dormo molto in treno. (*Guardando dal finestrino.*) Siamo a Torino.

Mario. Come si chiama questa regione d'It*a*lia? È bell*i*ssima.

Giovanni. Il Piemonte, è una regione montagnosa e collinosa. Fra due ore arriveremo a G*e*nova.

Mario. G*e*nova, la *Superba*!

Giovanni. Sa (Lei) perchè gl'Italiani la chi*a*mano la *Superba*?

Mario. No, perchè?

Giovanni. A c*a*usa delle ricchezze dei suoi bei palazzi.

Mario. È il primo porto commerciale d'It*a*lia, non è vero?

Giovanni. Sì, ed è molto importante. (*Apre lo sportello e va nel corridoio.*) Ma *e*ccoci quasi arrivati! Ora siamo in un'altra regione d'It*a*lia; la Lig*u*ria, e G*e*nova è al centro di questa regione, fra la Riviera di Levante e la Riviera di Ponente. Vede quelle grandi navi? Vanno fino all'Am*e*rica.

Mario. Partiamo di nuovo. Ecco un campanello!

Giovanni. Sarà ora di andare al vagone ristorante per la prima colazione. Dal finestrino avremo una bella vista del mare.

(*Segue*)

EXERCISES

A. Answer the following:

1. Ha dormito bene Giovanni?
2. In quale regione sono adesso?
3. Com'è questa regione?
4. Perchè gl'Italiani chi*a*mano G*e*nova la *Superba*?
5. Chi ha aperto lo sportello?
6. In quale regione si trova G*e*nova?
7. Quali sono le due Riviere?
8. Fino a dove vanno le grandi navi?
9. Dove vanno i viaggiatori quando il treno riparte?
10. Che fanno nel vagone ristorante?

B. Give the third persons singular and plural of the following verbs, in the conditional:

1. m*e*ttere
2. l*e*ggere
3. dovere
4. chi*u*dere
5. venire

C. Put into the plural:

1. l'*o*cchio celeste
2. la bocca
3. la gu*a*ncia
4. la m*o*glie
5. il dito
6. la mano
7. l'or*e*cchio
8. l'uovo
9. l'uomo
10. la città

D. Translate:

1. La stazione di G*e*nova è vicino al mare.
2. Alcuni viaggiatori vanno nel corrid*o*io.
3. Il treno sta per entrare nella stazione.
4. Lei ha chiuso il finestrino, perchè?
5. Sto guardando il mare.
6. Stiamo comprando una rivista italiana.
7. Quando verrà la mia amica?
8. Questa ragazza ha male al dito.
9. Ogni mano ha cinque dita.
10. Abbiamo gli occhi per vedere e le or*e*cchie per udire.

E. Translate:

1. I have a headache today.
2. This child has a toothache.
3. My friend has had a sore throat all day.
4. The heart is the vital organ of the human body.
5. This train is going as far as Genoa.
6. In an hour we shall be in Turin.
7. I like this scenery very much.
8. There are some large ships in this port.
9. That ship will go as far as America.
10. There is a beautiful view of the sea from this window.

LESSON XXII

Imperfect tense

This tense, sometimes called the past descriptive, describes what happened, or what used to happen, in the past. It is used:

(*a*) To express an incomplete or habitual action:

e.g. Il sole splendeva. *The sun was shining.*

Parlavo francese ogni giorno quando ero gi*o*vane.
I spoke French every day when I was young.

(*b*) To express what was happening when something else happened:

e.g. Carlo telefonava mentre io scrivevo.
Charles was telephoning while I was writing.

Il sole splendeva mentre noi viaggiavamo.
The sun was shining while we were travelling.

(*c*) For descriptive purposes:

e.g. Il mare era calmo. *The sea was calm.*

NOTE.—In English the word "would" is often used to describe habitual action:

e.g. Ogni mattina partiva alla stessa ora.
Every morning he would leave at the same time.

To form the imperfect tense add the following endings to the stem of the verb:

First conjugation	*Second conjugation*	*Third conjugation*
-avo	-evo	-ivo
-avi	-evi	-ivi
-ava	-eva	-iva
-avamo	-evamo	-ivamo
-avate	-evate	-ivate
-*a*vano	-*e*vano	-*i*vano

These endings are the same for all verbs, regular and irregular, with the exception of the auxiliary *e*ssere.

NOTE.—Verbs with a contracted infinitive add the above endings to the stem of the original infinitive:

e.g. dire (*contracted from* d*i*cere), dicevo
fare (*contracted from* f*a*cere), facevo

Imperfect Tense of the Model Verbs

PARLARE		V*E*NDERE	
parlavo	*I was speaking, I used to speak, I spoke*, etc.	vendevo	*I was selling, I used to sell, I sold*, etc.
parlavi		vendevi	
parlava		vendeva	
parlavamo		vendevamo	
parlavate		vendevate	
parl*a*vano		vend*e*vano	

CAPIRE

capivo	*I used to understand, I understood*, etc.
capivi	
capiva	
capivamo	
capivate	
cap*i*vano	

Imperfect Tense of the Auxiliaries

AVERE		*E*SSERE	
avevo	*I used to have, I had*, etc.	ero	*I used to be, I was*, etc.
avevi		eri	
aveva		era	
avevamo		eravamo	
avevate		eravate	
av*e*vano		*e*rano	

Irregular Verbs—*scegliere, sedere*

SC*E*GLIERE, *to choose*, *p.p.* scelto
SEDERE, *to sit*, *p.p.* seduto

PRESENT INDICATIVE

scelgo	siedo
scegli	siedi
sc*e*glie	siede
scegliamo	sediamo
scegliete	sedete
sc*e*lgono	si*e*dono

NOTE.—*sedersi* (to sit down) is conjugated like *sedere*:

mi siedo, etc.

Like all reflexive verbs, as stated in Lesson XII, *sedersi* is conjugated with e*ssere* in the compound tenses:

mi sono seduto (a) *I sat down*, etc.
ti sei seduto (a)
ci siamo seduti (e), *etc.*

VOCABULARY

esclamare	to exclaim
la vista	view
p*e*rdere di vista	to lose sight of
la galleria	tunnel
la spi*a*ggia	beach
la s*a*bbia	sand
l'ombra	shade, shadow
la pineta	pine wood, grove
il pino	pine tree
la passeggiata al mare	promenade
fare un bagno	to bathe
il bagno di sole	sun bathe
la carrozza	carriage
l'albergo	hotel
l'ascensore (*m.*)	lift
il molo	pier, quay
il caffè (*pl.* caffè)	café
il piano	floor, storey
al secondo piano	on the second floor
luminoso	luminous, clear
avvicinarsi	to approach, draw near
non vedere l'ora di	to long for
G*e*nova	Genoa
Santa Margherita	Santa Margherita
La Sp*e*zia	La Spezia
Viar*e*ggio	Viareggio
ad un tratto	all of a sudden
fine fine	very fine
l'uff*i*cio	office
la fontana	fountain
pieno	full
fra poco	soon, shortly
di tanto in tanto	now and then

DA G*E*NOVA A VIAR*E*GGIO

Molti viaggiatori *e*rano nel corrid*o*io e guard*a*vano il mare; ad un tratto M*a*rio esclamò.

Mario. Che bel mare! È tanto azzurro!

Giovanni. Di tanto in tanto questo bel mare sarà perduto di vista, ci sono tante gallerie fra G*e*nova e La Sp*e*zia.

Mario. Fra poco passeremo Santa Margherita, non è vero?

Giovanni. Sì, ed anche Rapallo e La Sp*e*zia, poi arriveremo a Viar*e*ggio.

Mario. È bella la spi*a*ggia de Viar*e*ggio?

Giovanni. È una delle più belle di queste parti, la s*a*bbia è fine fine. C'è anche una bella pineta dove potremo fare passeggiate all'ombra dei pini, quando farà troppo caldo al sole.

Mario. Non farà mai troppo caldo per me, non vedo l'ora di fare un bel bagno al mare e poi stare al sole. (*Si avvicinano alla stazione di Viareggio.*)

Giovanni. Ora siamo in Toscana. Il treno si ferma; dobbiamo sc*e*ndere s*u*bito. (*Prendono una carrozza e vanno all'albergo.*) Faremo una passeggiata stasera fino al Molo, vedrà la Fontana Luminosa, ed i bei Caffè pieni di gente; io facevo sempre una passeggiata dopo pranzo. (*Arrivano all'Albergo e prendono l'ascensore fino alle loro camere, al secondo piano.*)

(*Segue*)

EXERCISES

A. Answer the following:

1. Perchè sarà perduto di vista il mare?
2. Dove passerà fra poco il treno?
3. E poi dove arriveranno i viaggiatori?
4. È bella la spi*a*ggia di Viar*e*ggio?
5. Dove c'è una bella passeggiata all'ombra?
6. In quale regione si trova Viar*e*ggio?
7. Pr*e*ndono un tassì Giovanni e M*a*rio quando arr*i*vano alla stazione?
8. Dove vanno poi?
9. Che faranno la sera, dopo pranzo?
10. Che pr*e*ndono per arrivare alle loro c*a*mere?

B. Give the first persons singular and plural, imperfect tense, of the following verbs:

1. avere
2. *e*ssere
3. viaggiare
4. ric*e*vere
5. finire

C. Translate:

1. I used to do my work at the office.
2. What were you saying, John?
3. I was speaking to the porter.
4. This is a nice bedroom, is it not?
5. Yes, but the one I had before was more beautiful.

6. On what floor was it?
7. On the third, but the view from the window was magnificent.
8. This hotel is very modern.
9. It is not very big but it is comfortable (*comodo*).
10. Have you seen the fountain? No, not yet.

D. (*a*) Give the opposite of:

1. chiuso
2. perduto
3. bello
4. troppo caldo
5. all'ombra

(*b*) Put into the singular:

1. Questi alberghi moderni.
2. Quelle fontane luminose.
3. Delle passeggiate lunghe.
4. Degli studi diff*i*cili.
5. Quegli ascensori sono pieni.

E. Conjugate the following verbs in the imperfect tense:

(*a*) dire (*b*) andare (*c*) fare

LESSON XXIII

Use of the Definite Article

The definite article is required in Italian:

(*a*) Before a noun taken in a general sense.

e.g. I cavalli sono *u*tili. *Horses are useful.*

(*b*) Before abstract nouns.

e.g. La carità è una virtù. *Charity is a virtue.*

(*c*) Usually before surnames which are not preceded by the Christian name.

e.g. Un libro del Manzoni. *A book by Manzoni.*
(*Manzoni* being the surname)

BUT La Divina Comm*e*dia di Dante.
The Divine Comedy of Dante.
(*Dante* being a Christian name)

(*d*) It is also required when a title is followed by a proper name

e.g. Il professor Valli *Professor Valli*
Il signor Montani *Mr. Montani*

unless used in direct speech.

e.g. Come sta, signor Montani?
How are you, Mr. Montani?

Omission of the Definite Article

The definite article is omitted in Italian:

(*a*) Before a noun in apposition to another noun.

e.g. Londra, capitale d'Inghilterra
London, the capital of England

(*b*) Before an ordinal number used with a proper noun

e.g. Pio nono *Pius the Ninth*

Note how Italian differs from English in this respect.

Omission of the Indefinite Article

The indefinite article is omitted in Italian:

(*a*) Before a noun in apposition.

e.g. Piemonte, regione d'Italia
Piedmont, a province of Italy
Pisa, città toscana
Pisa, a town of Tuscany

(*b*) Before a noun in the predicate if it is unqualified.

e.g. Mio fratello è avvocato. *My brother is a lawyer.*
BUT Mio fratello è un buon avvocato.
My brother is a good lawyer.

(*c*) Also in exclamations after *che!* (What a . . . !)

e.g. Che bel tramonto! *What a lovely sunset!*
Che peccato! *What a pity!*

(*d*) As already stated, before *cento* and *mille*.

e.g. Ho cento francobolli. *I have one hundred stamps.*
Maria ha mille francobolli.
Mary has a thousand stamps.

Note how Italian differs from English in this respect also.

Irregular Verbs—*rispondere, scendere, crescere*

rispondere	*to answer*	*p.p.* risposto
scendere	*to descend*	*p.p.* sceso
crescere	*to grow*	*p.p.* cresciuto

The compound tenses of *rispondere* are conjugated with *avere*: ho risposto, *etc.*

Scendere and *crescere* are conjugated with *essere*:

sono sceso (a), *etc.*
sono cresciuto (a), *etc.*

NOTE.—If *crescere* is used as a transitive verb, meaning "to raise, bring up," it is conjugated with *avere*.

VOCABULARY

il soggiorno	stay, sojourn	la villa	country house
il mir*a*colo	miracle	all'aperto	in the open
il Battistero	Baptistry	cioè	that is, namely
la Torre Pendente	Leaning Tower	andare in torpedone, pullman	to go by coach
il campanile	bell tower	dec*i*dere	to decide
la meravi*g*lia	marvel, wonder	stabilire	to fix
il mondo	world	contenere	to contain
il p*u*lpito	pulpit	sembrare	to seem
il lampad*a*rio	chandelier	Gi*a*como Puccini (1858–1924)	
il pomer*i*ggio	afternoon	Galileo Galilei (1564–1642)	

PISA

Durante il loro soggiorno a Viar*e*ggio, M*a*rio e Giovanni dec*i*dono di fare una gita in torpedone fino a Pisa: in poco tempo arr*i*vano alla Piazza del Duomo.

Mario. Com'è bella questa Piazza!

Giovanni. Molti Italiani la chi*a*mano la Piazza dei Mir*a*coli, perchè contiene i tre bell*i*ssimi edifici, cioè: il Duomo, il Battistero e la Torre Pendente.

Mario. Con quel bel cielo azzurro e il prato verde sembra un vero mir*a*colo.

Giovanni. Questo campanile mi sembra una delle sette meravi*g*lie del mondo. (*Entrano nella Cattedrale.*)

Mario. Oh, quanto è bella e chiara! Che magn*i*fico p*u*lpito!

Giovanni. E quel lampad*a*rio di Galileo è superbo, non è vero? (*Dopo questa visita tutti e due salgono sulla Torre Pendente da dove hanno una bella veduta, poi fanno colazione in un ristorante vicino alla Piazza.*)

Giovanni. Questo pomer*i*ggio potremo andare a Torre del Lago.

Mario. Dov'è? È lontano?

Giovanni. È molto vicino! Potremo visitare la Villa di Gi*a*como Puccini. C'è un teatro all'aperto dove danno le sue *o*pere durante i mesi estivi.

Mario. Ho letto nel giornale stamattina che danno *La Bohème*. Potremo avere dei biglietti per stasera?

Giovanni. Andremo a vedere.

(*Segue*)

EXERCISES

A. Answer the following:

1. Che dec*i*dono di fare un giorno, Giovanni e M*a*rio, mentre sono a Viar*e*ggio?
2. È lontano Pisa da Viar*e*ggio?
3. Vanno in m*a*cchina?
4. Dove si ferma il torpedone quando arriva a Pisa?
5. Com'è chiamata questa piazza dagl'Italiani?
6. Quali tre edifici si tr*o*vano in questa piazza?
7. Dove *e*ntrano Giovanni e M*a*rio?
8. E poi quale edif*i*cio v*i*sitano?
9. Che fanno durante il pomer*i*ggio?
10. Dove si trova questa Villa?

B. Give the second persons singular and plural of the following verbs in the imperfect tense:

1. viaggiare
2. sc*e*ndere
3. partire
4. avere
5. *e*ssere

C. Translate:

1. Have you read this book by Manzoni?
2. I was speaking to Mr. Valli this morning.
3. How are you, signora Berti?
4. This Leaning Tower seems to us one of the seven wonders of the world.
5. Where is the villa of Giacomo Puccini?
6. It is in Torre del Lago, not far from Pisa.
7. Have you heard an Italian opera?
8. Yes, not only one but many.
9. Do you like the music of Puccini?
10. Yes, but my sister prefers the music of Giuseppe Verdi.

D. Translate:

1. While crossing the road.
2. Reading the newspaper.
3. Finding the hotel.
4. Leaving the station.
5. Finishing the dinner.

E. Translate:

1. Mio fratello è dottore.
2. Pisa, città toscana, non è lontano da Firenze.
3. La Toscana, regione d'It*a*lia, è molto bella.
4. Che peccato! Non c'è tempo di visitare il museo.
5. Ha risposto alla l*e*ttera, Roberto? No, non ancora.
6. Siamo scesi alla stazione di Viar*e*ggio.
7. La ragazza è cresciuta molto quest'anno.
8. Questi tre edifici sono magn*i*fici.

LESSON XXIV

Past Definite of Regular Verbs

The endings for the three conjugations are as follows:

First conjugation	*Second conjugation*	*Third conjugation*
-ai	-ei *or* -etti	-ii
-asti	-esti	-isti
-ò	-è *or* -ette	-ì
-ammo	-emmo	-immo
-aste	-este	-iste
-*a*rono	-*e*rono *or* -*e*ttero	-*i*rono

NOTE.—

(*a*) The accent on the last vowel of the third person singular in each of the conjugations; this is found in all regular verbs.

(*b*) Except for the *-ò* in the first conjugation the characteristic vowel of each conjugation is kept in all the persons.

(*c*) Some verbs in *-ere* have an alternative form for the first and third persons singular and the third person plural.

Past Definite of the Model Verbs

PARLARE,	*to speak*	V*E*NDERE,	*to sell*	CAPIRE,	*to understand*
parlai	*I spoke*, etc.	vendei *or* -etti	*I sold*, etc.	capii	*I understood*, etc.
parlasti		vendesti		capisti	
parlò		vendè *or* -ette		capì	
parlammo		vendemmo		capimmo	
parlaste		vendeste		capiste	
parl*a*rono		vend*e*rono *or* -*e*ttero		cap*i*rono	

Use of the Past Definite

This tense is used to express an action begun and completed at a definite time in the past. It is widely used in conversation, and for narration and historical events:

e.g. Dove andò mercoledì scorso?
Where did you go last Wednesday?
Tre anni fa comprai una villa.
Three years ago, I bought a country house.
Leonardo da Vinci morì nell'anno 1519.
Leonardo da Vinci died in 1519.

Prefixes

The prefixes most commonly used in Italian are:

(*a*) *dis-* (or simply *s-*) which usually gives the opposite meaning to the word to which it is joined:

e.g. fare *to do*; disfare *or* sfare *to undo, to dissolve.*
dire *to say, tell*; disdire *to cancel, to unsay.*
piacevole *pleasant, agreeable*;
spiacevole *unpleasant, disagreeable.*

(*b*) *ri-*, which implies repetition.

e.g. dire *to say*; ridire *to say again.*

(*c*) *stra-*, which intensifies the meaning of the word to which it is joined.

e.g. cotto (*p.p. of* cuocere, *to cook*), *cooked*;
stracotto *overcooked.*
vecchio *old*; stravecchio *very old.*

Suffixes

When a suffix is added to a word, the word is modified. Suffixes may be added to nouns, adjectives and adverbs. The suffixes most commonly used are:

(*a*) *-issimo*, added to adjectives and adverbs.

e.g. buono *good*; buonissimo *very good.*
bene *well*; benissimo *very well.*

NOTE.—The suffix is added to the word minus its final letter; the adjectives have a feminine form in *-a*.

(*b*) *-etto*, *-ino*, *-ello*, which are used as diminutives, or to denote endearment.

e.g. una casa *a house*; una casetta, una casina *a small* or *nice little house*.
un gatto *a cat*; un gattino *a small cat*, *kitten*.
un fiume *a river*: un fiumicello *a small river*.
caro *dear*; carino *little dear*, *darling*, *nice*.

(*c*) *-one*, fem. *-ona*, used as an augmentative.

e.g. un ragazzo *a boy*; un ragazzone *a big boy*.
una ragazza *a girl*; una ragazzona *a big girl*.

The feminine form *-ona* is only used for nouns which have a masculine and a feminine form.

Here are some feminine nouns which become masculine when the suffix *-ino* is added.

una tavola *a table*; un tavolino *a small table*.
una finestra *a window*; un finestrino *a small window*.
BUT una mano *a hand*; una manina *a tiny hand*.

VOCABULARY

la bottega	shop	il muro, *pl.* le mura	wall
il tesoro	treasure	Cimabue (1240–1302)	
l'arte	art	Dante Alighieri (1265–1321)	
la facciata	front, façade	Giotto (1276–1336)	
il marmo	marble	Brunelleschi (1377–1444)	
il capolavoro	masterpiece	Ghiberti (1378–1455)	
l'or*e*fice	goldsmith	Donatello (1386–1460)	
il cammeo	cameo	Michel*a*ngelo (1475–1564)	
l'orecchino	earring	Cellini (1500–1571)	
il ponte	bridge	creare	to create, produce
il Ponte V*e*cchio	famous bridge in Florence	n*a*scere	to be born
Santa Maria Novella, Santa Croce	churches in Florence	n*a*cque, n*a*cquero (*past def. of* n*a*scere)	(he) was born, (they) were born
il fiume	river		
l'Arno	river Arno		

fece (*past def. of* fare)	(he) made
il P*e*rseo	Perseus
degno	worthy
la pittura	painting
pian piano, lentamente	slowly
vidi (*past def. of* vedere)	(I) saw
bronzo	bronze
r*o*seo	rose-coloured, rosy
ricordare	to remember
il ricordo	remembrance, souvenir
lo scrittore	writer
l'architetto	architect
contenere	to contain

DA VIAR*E*GGIO A FIRENZE

Mentre Giovanni e M*a*rio vi*a*ggiano da Viar*e*ggio a Firenze in torpedone, amm*i*rano il paes*a*ggio.

Mario. È molto bello, questo paes*a*ggio. Dove siamo ora?

Giovanni. Vicino a Lucca. Vedrà, fra poco, le sue v*e*cchie mura ed alcuni bell*i*ssimi campanili.

Mario. Dov'è la cattedrale di Lucca?

Giovanni. Nella piazza di San Martino. La vedremo quando ci fermeremo.

Mario. È lontano di qui Firenze?

Giovanni. No, ci saremo fra un'ora.

Mario. Sarò tanto felice di vedere Firenze, è una città piena di tesori d'arte, non è vero?

Giovanni. Sì, il Duomo, il Battistero, con le sue famose porte di bronzo del Ghiberti, ed il Campanile di Giotto sono veri capolavori.

Mario. È di marmo la facciata del Duomo?

Giovanni. Sì, d'un marmo di bei colori, d'un colore r*o*seo e verde scuro.

Mario. Qual è la chiesa più bella ed antica di Firenze?

Giovanni. Santa Maria Novella è una delle più belle e antiche, e Santa Croce è famosa, come Lei sa.

Mario. Firenze è la p*a*tria di molti u*o*mini famosi, non è vero?

Giovanni. Sì, come Cimabue, maestro di Giotto, Dante, Brunelleschi, Donatello, Ghiberti e Michel*a*ngelo. Ma *e*ccoci arrivati, dobbiamo sc*e*ndere qui. Prenderemo una carrozza fino al Ponte V*e*cchio. Vedrà un po' della città, poi cammineremo sul Ponte, così vedrà le famose botteghe degli or*e*fici, e arriveremo pian piano alla Piazza del Duomo.

(*Segue*)

EXERCISES

A. Answer the following:

1. Che dice M*a*rio del paes*a*ggio fra Viar*e*ggio e Firenze?
2. In quale regione si tr*o*vano Pisa, Lucca e Firenze?
3. Com'è la facciata del Duomo di Firenze?
4. Su quale fiume è Firenze?
5. Ha veduto il Ponte V*e*cchio Lei?
6. Mi dica i nomi di due chiese di Firenze.
7. Sa dirmi il nome di un poeta fiorentino, molto famoso?
8. Sa dirmi i nomi di alcuni scultori e pittori?
9. Dove si tr*o*vano le p*i*ccole botteghe degli or*e*fici?
10. Perchè è famosa Firenze?

B. Give the third persons singular and plural of the following verbs in the past definite tense:

1. arrivare 2. v*e*ndere 3. preferire

C. Translate:

1. Dante was born in Florence.
2. Benvenuto Cellini, Giotto and Michelangelo were also born in this city.
3. These bronze doors are a masterpiece of art.
4. We are now near the bell tower of Giotto.
5. Last year I visited the Palazzo Vecchio and the Uffizi Galleries.

6. Florence gave to Italy many writers, poets, architects and artists.
7. This façade is really beautiful.
8. We bought some earrings and cameos from the little shops on the Ponte Vecchio.
9. These buildings are very old and the streets very narrow.
10. Tomorrow we will buy some souvenirs.

D. (*a*) Give the opposites of the following by using a prefix:

1. fare
2. dire
3. piac*e*vole
4. contento
5. obbedire

(*b*) Form diminutives from the following words:

1. un gatto
2. un fiasco
3. una casa
4. un fratello
5. una sorella

E. Translate:

Donatello creò *o*pere famose. Fece un Crocefisso di legno per la chiesa di Santa Croce a Firenze. Dante Alighieri fu (*was*) il più gran poeta d'It*a*lia. Quando andai a Firenze l'anno scorso, ammirai il P*e*rseo di Benvenuto Cellini. Vidi le porte di bronzo del Ghiberti, "degne di *e*ssere le porte del Paradiso,"—disse (*said*) Michel*a*ngelo. Questo monumento è il Campanile di Giotto. Quell'enorme edif*i*cio è la Galleria degli Uffizi, un museo che contiene una grande collezione di pitture.

LESSON XXV

Past Definite of Irregular Verbs

As already stated, most of the irregular verbs are only irregular in the past participle and the past definite, and of the past definite only three of the persons are irregular, viz. the first person singular, which always ends in *-i*, the third person singular, which always ends in *-e*, and the third person plural, which always ends in *-ero*.

The endings of the second person singular and the first and second persons plural are added to the stem of the infinitive, with the exception of *essere*, *dare* and *stare* which are very irregular.

PAST DEFINITE

VEDERE		DEC*I*DERE	
vidi	*I saw*, etc.	decisi	*I decided*, etc.
vedesti		decidesti	
vide		decise	
vedemmo		decidemmo	
vedeste		decideste	
v*i*dero		dec*i*sero	

M*E*TTERE		SCR*I*VERE	
misi	*I put*, etc.	scrissi	*I wrote*, etc.
mettesti		scrivesti	
mise		scrisse	
mettemmo		scrivemmo	
metteste		scriveste	
m*i*sero		scr*i*ssero	

Note that there is no accent on the third person singular of an irregular verb in this tense.

AVERE		*E*SSERE	
ebbi	*I had*, etc.	fui	*I was*, etc.
avesti		fosti	
ebbe		fu	
avemmo		fummo	
aveste		foste	
*e*bbero		f*u*rono	

DARE		STARE	
diedi *or* detti	*I gave*, etc.	stetti	*I stayed, stood, was,* etc.
desti		stesti	
diede *or* dette		stette	
demmo		stemmo	
deste		steste	
di*e*dero *or* d*e*ttero		st*e*ttero	

Idiomatic Uses of Prepositions

1. *da* ("by, from") also has the following meanings:

(*a*) "to" ("to the house *or* shop of").

e.g. Vado da Roberto. *I am going to Robert's house.*
Andiamo da lui, lei, loro.
Let us go to his, her, their house.

But note the following:

Vado da me. *I am going by myself.*
Vado a casa mia. *I am going home, to my house.*

(*b*) "with", describing a personal characteristic.

e.g. una ragazza dai capelli neri *a girl with black hair*

(*c*) It also indicates purpose

e.g. una tazza da caffè *a coffee cup*

2. *per* ("for") also translates "by, by means of".

e.g. per telegramma *by telegram* per via aerea *by air*
due per quattro *two by (multiplied by) four*

3. *in* ("in") used before countries, translates "to".

e.g. Vado in It*a*lia. *I am going to Italy.*

Note also:

Vado in città. *I am going to town.*

4. *a* (" to, at") has the following meanings:

   (*a*) "in" before a town.
   e.g. Abito a Firenze. *I live in Florence.*

   (*b*) It also implies the way in which something is done.
   e.g. chi*u*dere a chiave *to lock*, lit. *to close with a key*
   alla romana *in the Roman way*
   due a due *two by two*

5. *fra* or *tra* ("between, among") before time in the future is translated "in, soon".

   e.g. fra un'ora *in an hour*
   fra poco *soon*

6. *di* ("of") before adverbs is translated "from".

   e.g. lontano di qui *far from here*

   When referring to certain times of the day or year it is translated "in" or "by".

   e.g. di mattina, di sera, di notte, di giorno
   in the morning, *evening*, *by night*, *by day*

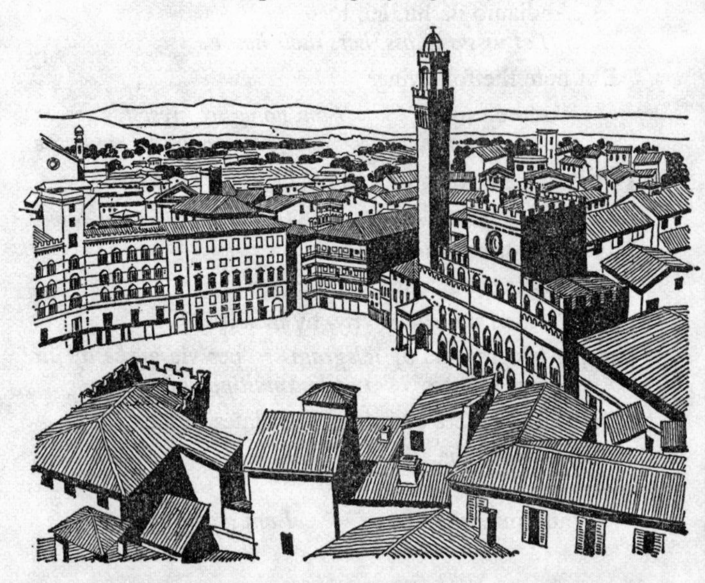

VOCABULARY

la corsa	race	medioevale	medieval
il P*a*lio	piece of rich cloth given as a prize (*fig.* race, prize)	v*a*rio	various
		peccato!	too bad!
		che peccato!	what a pity!
il fantino	jockey	rappresentare	to represent
il costume	costume	aver luogo	to take place
il quartiere	district	tre mesi fa	three months ago
il campo	field, ground	però	however
il Campo	large Square	Elena	Helen
l'album (*m.*)	scrapbook, album		

SIENA

Giovanni. Domani andremo a Siena; come Lei sa è una città molto antica e bella. Non ci sarà la Corsa del P*a*lio, però, domani.

*M*a*rio.* Che cosa è la Corsa del P*a*lio?

Giovanni. È una corsa di cavalli alla quale pr*e*ndono parte numerosi fantini, tutti vestiti in costumi medioevali che rappres*e*ntano i differenti quartieri di Siena.

Mario. E quando ha luogo questa corsa?

Giovanni. Due volte l'anno, il due l*u*glio ed il s*e*dici agosto.

*M*a*rio.* E dove?

Giovanni. Nella grande piazza chiamata il Campo.

*M*a*rio.* Dev'*e*ssere interessante questa corsa! È bello il Duomo di Siena?

Giovanni. Molto, la sua facciata è di marmo rosso, bianco e nero.

*M*a*rio.* Quante volte è stato a Siena, Lei?

Giovanni. Questa sarà la mia seconda v*i*sita.

(*Segue*)

EXERCISES

A. Answer the following:

1. Dove arriv*a*rono il giorno seguente M*a*rio e Giovanni?
2. È mai stato a Siena, Lei?
3. Com'è chiamata la corsa a Siena?
4. Dove e quando ha luogo?
5. Come si chiama questa Piazza?
6. Chi prende parte a questa corsa?

7. Come sono vestiti i fantini?
8. Com'è la facciata del Duomo?
9. In quale regione si trova Siena?
10. Le piacerebbe visitare questa città?

B. (*a*) Supply the correct form of the past definite of the following verbs in brackets:

1. Maria (finire) il suo lavoro.
2. Noi (v*e*ndere) la m*a*cchina.
3. Essi (fare) una passeggiata.
4. Io (andare) a Pisa tre anni fa.
5. Voi (arrivare) troppo tardi.

(*b*) Translate the words in brackets:

1. Andammo al mare (*two months ago*).
2. (*Sometimes*) visitavamo il museo.
3. (*Often*) parlavamo del vi*a*ggio.
4. (*What a pity*) ho perduto il treno.
5. Ho quasi (*one thousand*) francobolli nel mio album.

C. Translate the completed sentences in Exercise B.

D. Translate the following conversation:

Where are you going, Margaret and Helen?
We are going to town, do you want to come with us?
No thanks, I must go to my sister's house now.
Where does she live?
In Trent Road, number eleven.
When is she leaving for Milan?
Next week, by air.
What are you going to buy, Helen?
Some coffee cups for my cousins.
And I will buy some teaspoons.

E. Continue the following verbs in the past definite tense:

1. l*e*ggere: lessi, leggesti, *etc*.
2. chi*e*dere: chiesi, chiedesti, *etc*.
3. chi*u*dere: chiusi, chiudesti, *etc*.
4. dire: dissi, dicesti, *etc*.
5. m*e*ttere: misi, mettesti, *etc*.

LESSON XXVI

Comparison of Adjectives

There are three degrees of comparison of an adjective:

1. The positive, which is the adjective in its simple form.
2. The comparative, which expresses a higher or a lower degree; this is formed by placing *più* (more) or *meno* (less) before the adjective.
3. (*a*) The superlative relative, which expresses the highest or the lowest degree; this is formed by placing the definite article in front of *più* or *meno*.

   (*b*) The superlative absolute, which expresses a very high or a very low degree, without any suggestion of comparison; this is formed by adding *-issimo*, *-issima*, *-issimi*, *-issime*, to the adjective, after the final vowel has been dropped.

A. *Comparisons of Equality*

In Italian comparisons of equality are formed in the following way:

così . . . come	*as, so . . . as*
tanto . . . quanto	*as much . . . as*

e.g. Roberto è così ricco come Lorenzo
or Roberto è ricco come Lorenzo.
Robert is as rich as Lawrence.

Pietro non è tanto coraggioso quanto Paolo
or Pietro non è coraggioso quanto Paolo.
Peter is not as brave as Paul.

Note that *così* and *tanto* may be omitted.

B. *Comparisons of Inequality*

In comparisons the word "than" is translated by *di* or *che*.
di is used before a noun, a pronoun *or* a number:

e.g. Carlo è più alto di Luigi. *Charles is taller than Louis.*
Caterina è più alta di me. *Catherine is taller than I.*

Francesco ha più di mille francobolli.
Francis has more than one thousand stamps.

NOTE.—If there are two nouns used without an article in a general sense and both of them are subjects *or* objects of the same verb, "than" is translated by *che*.

e.g. C'è più latte che caffè in questa tazza.
There is more milk than coffee in this cup.

che is used before all other parts of speech:

e.g. (*a*) *Adverbs.*
Meglio tardi che mai.
Better late than never.

(*b*) *Verbs.*
Preferisco suonare che cantare.
I prefer playing to singing.

(*c*) *Prepositions.*
Ci sono più sigarette in questo pacchetto che in quella sc*a*tola.
There are more cigarettes in this packet than in that box.

(*d*) *Adjectives.*
Questa ragazza è più studiosa che intelligente.
This girl is more studious than intelligent.

Comparisons in which *tanto* is used as an adjective require that *quanto* also agrees with the noun:

e.g. tanta (*f.sing.*) . . . quanta	*as much . . . as*
tanti (*m.pl.*) . . . quanti	*as many . . . as*
tante (*f.pl.*) . . . quante	

Maria ha tanta pazienza quanta sua madre.
Mary has as much patience as her mother.

Giovanni ha tanti libri quanti Roberto.
John has as many books as Robert.
Ho tante cugine quante lui.
I have as many cousins as he.

TABLE OF COMPARISONS

Positive	Comparative	Superlative Relative	Superlative Absolute
caro *dear, expensive*	più caro meno caro *more dear, dearer* *less dear, cheaper*	il più caro il meno caro *the most dear, dearest* *the least dear, cheapest*	car*issimo* *very dear*

NOTE.—Adjectives which end in *-co* or *-go* insert *h* between *c* or *g* and *-issimo* in order to keep the hard sound:

e.g. ricco *rich* ricch*issimo* *very rich*
lungo *long* lungh*issimo* *very long*

Note the following six adjectives which have both regular and irregular forms:

Positive		Comparative		Superlative Relative		Superlative Absolute	
buono	*good*	più buono *or* migliore	*better*	il più buono *or* il migliore	*the best*	buon*issimo* *or* ottimo	*very good*
cattivo	*bad*	più cattivo *or* peggiore	*worse*	il più cattivo *or* il peggiore	*the worst*	cattiv*issimo* *or* pessimo	*very bad*
grande	*big, great*	più grande *or* maggiore	*bigger, greater*	il più grande *or* il maggiore	*biggest, greatest*	grand*issimo* *or* massimo	*very big*
piccolo	*small*	più piccolo *or* minore	*smaller*	il più piccolo *or* il minore	*smallest*	piccol*issimo* *or* minimo	*very small*
alto	*high*	più alto *or* superiore	*higher*	il più alto *or* il superiore	*the highest*	alt*issimo* *or* supremo	*very high*
basso	*low*	più basso *or* inferiore	*lower*	il più basso *or* l'inferiore	*the lowest*	infimo	*very low*

NOTE.—*Maggiore* and *minore* signify also "older" and "younger". Use *superiore* and *inferiore* for quality, etc.

Comparison of Adverbs

The comparative and superlative forms of adverbs are formed in exactly the same way as those of adjectives, e.g.:

Positive	*Comparative*	*Superlative Relative*	*Superlative Absolute*
riccamente *richly*	più riccamente	il più riccamente	ricchissimamente

Irregular Comparison of Adverbs

Positive		*Comparative*		*Superlative Relative*		*Superlative Absolute*	
bene	*well*	meglio	*better*	il meglio	*the best*	ottimanente	*very well*
male	*badly*	peggio	*worse*	il peggio	*the worst*	pessimamente	*very badly*
molto	*much*	più	*more*	il più	*the most*	molt*i*ssimo	*very much*
poco	*little*	meno	*less*	il meno	*the least*	poch*i*ssimo	*very little*

NOTE.—Adjectives and adverbs are sometimes repeated to form the superlative absolute:

e.g. rosso rosso	*very red*
piano piano *or* pian piano	*very slowly, gently*

VOCABULARY

la Città Eterna	Eternal City	San Giovanni in Laterano	St. John Lateran
la capitale	capital	la bas*i*lica	basilica
il Colosseo	Colosseum	volere	to want
il Foro	Forum	dimenticare	to forget
la Fontana di Trevi	Fountain of Trevi	buttare	to throw
la pir*a*mide	pyramid	prenotare	to book (seats)
Porta San P*a*olo	Saint Paul's Gate	div*i*dere	to divide
Teatro di Caracalla	Caracalla Theatre	si dice	it is said (they say)
lo spett*a*colo	scene, sight	pr*a*tica	practical
San Pietro	St. Peter	il soldo	soldo (*fig.* copper, penny, etc.)
Santa Maria Maggiore	St. Mary the Greater, Major	Parigi	Paris
San P*a*olo fuori le Mura	St. Paul outside the walls	avverato	proved, come true
		il sogno	dream

ROMA

Giovanni e M*a*rio pr*e*ndono il treno per Roma e arr*i*vano verso mezzogiorno.

Giovanni. *E*ccoci a Roma, la Città Eterna.

Mario. Che bella stazione e com'è grande e moderna!

Giovanni. È la nuova stazione T*e*rmini; sì, è veramente bella e molto pr*a*tica.

Mario. Ho sempre voluto visitare la capitale d'It*a*lia. In quale regione siamo ora?

Giovanni. Nel L*a*zio. Roma si può div*i*dere in tre parti. Roma antica, Roma medioevale e Roma moderna.

Mario. Quali sono le quattro bas*i*liche importanti di Roma?

Giovanni. San Pietro, che è la Cattedrale più grande del mondo, San Giovanni in Laterano, Santa Maria Maggiore, e San P*a*olo fuori le Mura.

Mario. Visiteremo tutt'e quattro, più tardi, non è vero?

Giovanni. Certo; c'è tanto da vedere a Roma—ma abbiamo tempo.

Mario. Sì, è vero. Roma è famosa non solo per le chiese, il Colosseo ed il Foro ma anche, si dice, per la bellezza delle sue fontane.

Giovanni. Vedremo facilmente le fontane perchè sono quasi tutte in grandi piazze—e non dobbiamo dimenticare di buttare un soldo nella fontana di Trevi.

Mario. Perchè?

Giovanni. Perchè si dice che chi farà così sarà certo di rivedere la Città Eterna. Sa che c'è una pir*a*mide a Roma?

Mario. No, non sapevo ciò, dove?

Giovanni. Vicino a Porta San P*a*olo; la vedremo domani prima di andare alla bas*i*lica di San P*a*olo.

Mario. Potremo andare, una sera, al Teatro di Caracalla?

Giovanni. Sì, prenoteremo biglietti per un'*o*pera; nel giornale ci sarà il programma, e vedremo quale *o*pera daranno domani. Questo Teatro è all'aperto, come Lei sa.

Mario. Sarà per me uno spett*a*colo meraviglioso, un sogno avverato.

(*Segue*)

EXERCISES

A. Answer the following:

1. A che ora arr*i*vano a Roma i nostri viaggiatori?
2. In quale regione sono ora?
3. Quali sono le quattro famose bas*i*liche di Roma?
4. Quali visiteranno Giovanni e M*a*rio?
5. Che faranno quando visiteranno la fontana di Trevi?
6. Perchè?
7. C'è una pir*a*mide a Roma?
8. Dove?
9. Le piacerebbe visitare questa capitale?
10. Qual è la capitale della Fr*a*ncia?

11. Qual è la capitale dell'Inghilterra?
12. Quali capitali ha Lei visitate?

B. Give the first and third persons plural of the following verbs in the conditional tense:

1. l*e*ggere
2. dire
3. visitare
4. fare
5. partire

C. Translate:

1. Luigi speaks Italian better than Paul.
2. This book is the best of the three.
3. This is a very good idea.
4. Charles is the eldest.
5. Helen is the youngest.
6. That tower is higher than this one.
7. Three days ago I saw a wonderful view.
8. Unfortunately I could not take a photograph of it.
9. Peter is as tall as Paul.
10. Robert is the tallest.

D. (*a*) Give the opposites of the following:

1. maggiore
2. superiore
3. m*e*glio
4. *o*ttimo
5. bene

(*b*) Give the superlative absolute of the following:

1. p*i*ccolo
2. poco
3. alto
4. molto
5. bene

E. Revise all the tenses studied so far of the auxiliary verbs, and write the third persons singular and plural of each tense.

LESSON XXVII

The Subjunctive Mood

The subjunctive is used to express an action which may be possible but is uncertain. This action is generally dependent on another action. The subjunctive is mainly found in a subordinate clause when the verb in the main clause expresses fear, doubt, emotion, opinion, etc.

e.g. Temo che questo ragazzo *a*bbia un raffreddore.
I fear this child has a cold.
Mi dispiace che Lei non stia bene.
I am sorry you are not well.

Note, however, that the subjunctive is not used when the subject in both clauses is the same; in this case the infinitive is used:

e.g. Temo d'arrivare troppo tardi.
I fear I may arrive too late.

PRESENT SUBJUNCTIVE

PARLARE		VENDERE	
parli	(*that*) *I may speak*, etc.	venda	(*that*) *I may sell*, etc.
parli		venda	
parli		venda	
parliamo		vendiamo	
parliate		vendiate	
p*a*rlino		v*e*ndano	

CAPIRE		PARTIRE	
capisca	(*that*) *I may understand*, etc.	parta	(*that*) *I may leave*, *depart*, etc.
capisca		parta	
capisca		parta	
capiamo		partiamo	
capiate		partiate	
cap*i*scano		p*a*rtano	

Verbs in *-ire* which do not have the *-isc-* in the present indicative are conjugated like *partire*.

Here are a few verbs conjugated like *capire*:

apparire	*to appear*	condire	*to season*
costruire	*to build*	digerire	*to digest*
guarire	*to cure*	preferire	*to prefer*
pulire	*to clean*	finire	*to finish*

and here are some conjugated like *partire*:

consentire	*to agree*	sentire	*to hear or smell*
divertire	*to amuse*	sentirsi	*to feel*
divertirsi	*to enjoy oneself*	soffrire	*to suffer*
seguire	*to follow*	vestire	*to dress*

Present Subjunctive of the Auxiliaries

	AVERE		*E*SSERE
*a*bbia	(*that*) *I may have*,	sia	(*that*) *I may be*,
*a*bbia	etc.	sia	etc.
*a*bbia		sia	
abbiamo		siamo	
abbiate		siate	
*a*bbiano		s*i*ano	

NOTE.—Verbs in the present subjunctive have the same form for the three persons singular.

The subjunctive is also used:

(*a*) After certain conjunctions such as *sebbene*, *benchè* (although), *affinchè* (in order that), *a meno che* (unless), *prima che* (before), and a few others.

e.g. Sebbene *or* benchè egli sia ricco non è felice.
Although he is rich he is not happy.
Prima che Roberto parta telefona sempre al suo amico.
Before Robert leaves he always telephones his friend.

(*b*) After a superlative relative and also after *primo*, u*ltimo* and u*nico*:

e.g. È il più p*i*ccolo cane ch'io *a*bbia mai visto.
It is the smallest dog I have ever seen.

(*c*) After certain indefinite words such as *chiunque* (whoever), *qualunque* (whatever), etc.

VOCABULARY

il giovanotto	young man	la fetta	slice
il gelato	ice-cream	il panino	roll (bread)
la caramella	boiled sweet	il pacchetto	small parcel
il cestino	small basket	il fiaschetto	small flask
il cestino da vi*a*ggio	lunch-basket, packed lunch	la gente	people
il tovagliolo	serviette	perfino	even
le lasagne	(broad) strips of macaroni	lasciare	to leave
il sale	salt	gridare	to shout, cry out
la porzione	portion	il raffreddore	cold, chill
il pollo	chicken	il marciapiede	pavement, (*station*) platform

DA ROMA A MILANO

Giovanni. Ora lasciamo il L*a*zio e quando passeremo per Orvieto saremo in *U*mbria, poi, poco dopo, di nuovo nella Toscana.

Mario. È lungo il vi*a*ggio da Roma a Milano, non è vero?

Giovanni. Sì, dura otto ore. Questo treno non si ferma tante volte.

Mario. A quali stazioni si ferma?

Giovanni. Credo che Orvieto, Firenze, Bologna e Parma s*i*ano le stazioni principali.

Mario. In quale regione si trova Bologna?

Giovanni. In Em*i*lia.

Mario. E Milano?

Giovanni. In Lombardia.

(*I due viaggiatori leggono i giornali. Il treno arriva alla stazione di Bologna e si ferma. Dei giovanotti sul marciapiede, gridano: gelati, caramelle, frutta, cestini da viaggio!*)

Giovanni. Non sarebbe una buon'idea comprare due cestini invece di andare al vagone ristorante?

Mario. Certo, costeranno meno di un pranzo in treno.

Giovanni. E sono sempre buoni!

(*Comprano due cestini, e il treno riparte.*)

Mario. Vorrei sapere che c'è in questo cestino.

Giovanni (*aprendo il suo*). Un piatto caldo di lasagne con una forchetta, pollo, due fette di prosciutto, panini, formaggio, frutta, un fiaschetto di vino, e perfino un pacchettino di sale ed un tovagliolo di carta.

Mario. Anch'io ho lo stesso nel mio. Buon appetito!

Giovanni. Grazie, altrettanto a Lei.

(*Cominciano a mangiare.*)

(*Segue*)

EXERCISES

A. Answer the following:

1. In quale regione si trova Orvieto?
2. È lungo il viaggio da Roma a Milano?
3. Come passano il tempo i nostri viaggiatori?
4. Che gridano alcuni giovanotti alla stazione di Bologna?
5. Che comprano Giovanni e Mario?
6. Che trovano nei cestini da viaggio?
7. Le piace il prosciutto?
8. Le piacciono i gelati?
9. Che dice Mario a Giovanni prima di cominciare a mangiare?
10. Che risponde Giovanni?

B. Put into the subjunctive:

1. Lei ha
2. essi sono
3. io finisco
4. Loro vendono
5. io sono
6. voi vendete
7. Loro partono
8. io preferisco
9. tu hai
10. Lei compra

C. Translate:

1. I hope you are well.
2. We fear Robert is ill.
3. These people are rich but they are not happy.
4. Although Charles and Peter are poor they are very happy.
5. Have you visited Rome before?
6. No, this is the first time I have been (*say* am) here.
7. Do you think Peter will come tomorrow?
8. No, I think he has gone to London.
9. I have brought you a flask of white wine.
10. You are very kind, thank you very much.

D. Conjugate in the subjunctive the following verbs:

1. avere
2. *e*ssere
3. cantare
4. ric*e*vere
5. finire

E. Revise all tenses of the indicative mood of the model verbs and write the second persons singular and plural of each tense.

LESSON XXVIII

The Imperative Mood

The imperative is used when one asks or commands someone to do something. It is really only used in the second persons singular and plural and the first person plural:

e.g. Parla italiano. *Speak Italian.*
Parliamo italiano. *Let us speak Italian.*
Parlate italiano. *Speak Italian.*

As there is no imperative form for *Lei* and *Loro*, it is supplied from the third persons singular and plural of the present subjunctive:

e.g. Finisca il Suo lavoro. *Finish your work.*
M*a*ndino queste cartoline ai Loro amici.
Send these postcards to your friends.

PARLARE

Second person singular	parla	*speak* (tu *understood*)
Third person singular	parli	*speak* (Lei *understood*)
First person plural	parliamo	*let us speak*
Second person plural	parlate	*speak* (voi *understood*)
Third person plural	parlino	*speak* (Loro *understood*)

V*E*NDERE	FINIRE	PARTIRE
vendi	finisci	parti
venda	finisca	parta
vendiamo	finiamo	partiamo
vendete	finite	partite
v*e*ndano	fin*i*scano	p*a*rtano

NOTE.—The first and second persons plural of the imperative are the same as the first and second persons plural of the present indicative minus the pronouns, except in the cases of *avere* and e*ssere*, where the second person plural is the same as the subjunctive, and *sapere* and *volere*.

AVERE	ESSERE
abbi	sii
abbia	sia
abbiamo	siamo
abbiate	siate
abbiano	siano

NOTE.—Except in the second person singular, the imperative is made negative in the usual way, by the use of *non*:

e.g. Non parli. *Do not speak.*
Non parliamo. *Do not let us speak.*
Non parlate. *Do not speak.*
Non parlino. *Do not speak.*

But to form the imperative negative of the second person singular, the *infinitive* is used, preceded by *non*:

e.g. Non parlare *Do not speak.*
Non vendere. *Do not sell.*
Non finire. *Do not finish.*

When used with the imperative affirmative in the second person singular and the first and second persons plural, the conjunctive pronouns (except *loro* and *Loro*) are joined to it and form one word:

e.g. Compra quella casa. *Buy that house.*
BUT Comprala. *Buy it.*
Compriamola. *Let us buy it.*
Compratela. *Buy it.*

When used with the imperative negative, the pronouns may precede or follow the verb:

e.g. Non la comprare.
Non comprarla. } *Do not buy it.*
Non la compriamo. *Do not let us buy it.*

NOTE.—With the polite form of the imperative the pronouns (except *loro* and *Loro*) *precede* the verb, when used either affirmatively or negatively:

e.g. *sing. form:* La compri, signora. *Buy it, madam.*
Non la compri, signora. *Do not buy it, madam.*

pl. form:	La comprino, signorine.	*Buy it, ladies.*
	Non la comprino, signorine.	*Do not buy it, ladies.*
sing. form:	Parli loro.	*Speak to them.*
	Non parli loro.	*Do not speak to them.*
pl. form:	Parlino loro.	*Speak to them.*
	Non parlino loro.	*Do not speak to them.*

There are three other cases in which the conjunctive pronouns are joined to the verb in the same way as in the imperative affirmative, viz:

(*a*) The infinitive, as already stated in Lesson IX:

e.g. Vado a comprarla. *I am going to buy it* (*f.*).
È pericoloso sporgersi.
It is dangerous to lean out (*i.e. of the window*).

(*b*) The gerund:

e.g. vedendola *seeing it* (or *her*)

(*c*) The past participle when used without an auxiliary verb:

e.g. Ho comprato una casa. *I have bought a house.*

BUT Compratola sono molto felice.
Having bought it, I am very happy.

If the imperative consists of one syllable only (e.g. *da'* (give), *fa'* (do, make), the initial letter of the pronoun joined to it is doubled:

e.g. dammi *give me*; fammi *do me, make me.*

Dalle subito il telegramma.
Give her the telegram at once.

Gli, however, is an exception to this rule:

e.g. dagli *give him*

Loro is never attached to the verb:

e.g. da' loro *give them*

Table of Conjunctive Pronouns

Subject		*Direct object*		*Indirect object*		*Reflexive*	
io	*I*	mi	*me*	mi	*to me*	mi	*myself*
tu	*you*	ti	*you*	ti	*to you*	ti	*yourself*
egli, lui	*he*	lo	*him, it*	gli	*to him, it*	si	*himself, itself*
ella, lei	*she*	la	*her, it*	le	*to her, it*	si	*herself, itself*
Lei	*you*	La	*you*	Le	*to you*	si	*yourself*
noi	*we*	ci	*us*	ci	*to us*	ci	*ourselves*
voi	*you*	vi	*you*	vi	*to you*	vi	*yourselves*
essi	*they*	li	*them*	loro	*to them*	si	*themselves*
esse	*they*	le	*them*	loro	*to them*	si	*themselves*
Loro	*you*	Li, Le	*you*	Loro	*to you*	si	*yourselves*

ne, *some*, *any*, *of it*, *some of it*, etc.

Double Conjunctive Pronouns

When two conjunctive pronouns are governed by the same verb and one is the *direct* and the other the *indirect object*, the *indirect* precedes the *direct object*.

Both these pronouns either precede or follow the verb according to the rules already stated for the single pronoun.

NOTE.—(*a*) the *i* of *mi*, *ti*, *si*, *ci* and *vi* is changed to *e* when followed by a direct object pronoun (*lo*, *la*, *li*, *le*, *ne*):

e.g. Carlo me lo darà. *Charles will give it to me.*

(*b*) *gli* (to him) and *le* (to her, to you) become *glie* and are written as one word with the pronoun which follows, thus giving these forms:

glielo, gliela } *it to him, it to her, it to you*
glieli, gliele } *them to him, them to her, them to you*
gliene *some to him, some to her, some to you*

(*c*) *Loro* and *loro*, as always, follow the verb:

e.g. Lo do loro. *I give it to them.*

Conjunctive Adverbs

"Here", "there" and "in it", when referring to a place already mentioned and not used emphatically, are translated by *ci* or *vi*. "From there" and "thence" are translated by *ne*:

e.g. È Lei stato a Londra questa settimana? Sì, ci andai due giorni fa.
Have you been to London this week? Yes, I went there two days ago.

Viene spesso a Lucca, Margherita? Sì, ci vengo ogni anno.
Do you often come to Lucca, Margaret? Yes, I come here every year.

Maria uscì dalla casa alle dieci, io ne uscii a mezzogiorno.
Mary went out of the house at ten o'clock, I went out from there at noon.

NOTE.—These adverbs, used only in connection with a verb, precede or follow the verb according to the rules studied for the conjunctive pronouns above:

e.g. Devo ritornarci. *I must return there.*
Uscendone . . . *Going out from there . . .*

VOCABULARY

la scala	staircase, stairs
la scala m*o*bile	moving staircase, escalator
la *Scala*	Scala Theatre
la Galleria	famous shopping arcade
la g*u*glia	spire
l'ottava meravi*g*lia	eighth wonder
l'*U*ltima Cena, il Cen*a*colo	Last Supper
l'esterno	exterior, outside
l'interno	interior, inside
lo stile	style
il caffè, l'espresso	strong (black) coffee
il cappuccino	coffee with frothed-up milk
il caffè e latte *or* caffèlatte	coffee with milk
Santa Maria delle Gr*a*zie	(famous church in Milan)
Leonardo da Vinci (1452–1519)	
Castello Sforzesco	Sforza Castle
il lato	side
notare	to note, notice
la coincidenza	connection (railway), coincidence
l'or*a*rio	timetable
g*o*tico	gothic

MILANO

Mario. Ecco la stazione centrale di Milano.

Giovanni. Vedrà che è una stazione molto ornata, ma non piace a tutti. Scenderemo la scala di marmo, vedrà anche una scala m*o*bile. Prima di uscire, prenderemo un caffè, o un cappuccino. Che preferisce?

Mario. Un espresso, per favore. Quante ore avremo a Milano?

Giovanni. Almeno quattro, ma vedremo l'or*a*rio fra poco.

Mario. *E*ccolo! Treni in Arrivo . . . Treni in Partenza . . . Ah, ecco! . . . Milano-Vene*z*ia.

Giovanni. La coincidenza per Vene*z*ia sarà alle ore diciannove.

Mario. Così avremo quasi cinque ore qui.

Giovanni. E poi, ritornando da Venezia, altre cinque ore; così potrà vedere un po' di questa città industriale. Sarebbe meglio prendere *su*bito un tassì fino alla Piazza del Duomo.

Mario. Per vedere prima il famoso Duomo di Milano? Che stile è?

Giovanni. È di stile gotico, e Lei sa che è tutto di marmo, non è vero?

Mario. Sì. Quante st*a*tue ci sono sul Duomo?

Giovanni. Più di duemila st*a*tue e centotrentacinque g*u*glie.

Mario. Ora capisco perchè i Milanesi chi*a*mano questa cattedrale "L'ottava meraviglia del mondo"!

Giovanni. Mi dispiace che non ci sia tempo oggi per vedere l'*U*ltima Cena, di Leonardo da Vinci, ma ritornando da Venezia, avremo altre cinque ore a Milano, e così vedrà questo bel capolavoro.

Mario. Dove si trova?

Giovanni. Nella chiesa di Santa Maria delle Gr*a*zie, ma sarà chiusa a quest'ora.

Mario. Potremo vedere La Scala?

Giovanni. Soltanto l'esterno—anch'essa sarà chiusa.

Mario. È lontano dal Duomo?

Giovanni. No, è dall'altro lato della famosa Galleria.

Mario. Dov'è il Castello Sforzesco?

Giovanni. *E*ccolo.

(*Fanno un giro della città in tassì, poi ritornano alla stazione e prendono il treno per Venezia.*)

(*Segue*)

EXERCISES

A. Answer the following:

1. Piace a tutti la stazione di Milano?
2. Che prendono M*a*rio e Giovanni prima di uscire dalla stazione?
3. A che serve un or*a*rio?
4. Vanno a piedi fino alla piazza del Duomo?
5. Di che stile è il Duomo di Milano?

6. Quante st*a*tue ci sono su questo Duomo?
7. Come lo chi*a*mano i Milanesi?
8. Dove si trova l'*U*ltima Cena di Leonardo da Vinci?
9. È lontano dalla Piazza del Duomo La Scala?
10. Quale Castello v*e*dono prima di ritornare alla stazione?

B. Give all the imperative forms of *avere*, *e*ss*ere*, *cantare*, *ric*e*vere* and *finire*.

C. Translate:

1. Show me that book, please, Charles.
2. Bring me those newspapers, Mary.
3. Pass him that letter.
4. Show me your books, children.
5. Have you the postcard from Mr. Valli? Give it to John, please.

D. Put into the negative:

1. Compra quel tavolino.
2. Parli a quell'uomo.
3. Mangiamo all'albergo.
4. Vendi la tua casetta.
5. P*a*rtano prima delle *u*ndici.

E. Substitute the words in brackets with a pronoun:

1. Ecco (la pittura).
2. Mostri (la pir*a*mide).
3. Ammirando (il campanile).
4. Vedo (i fiori) laggiù.
5. Parlo (a Roberto).
6. Scriviamo (a Rita).
7. Ecco (i giardini).
8. Devo visitare (il museo).
9. Non scrivo (alle signorine).
10. Chiama (il cameriere), per favore.

F. (*a*) Translate into English:

1. Gliene parleremo.
2. Carlo glieli mandò.
3. Maria me ne comprerà.
4. Glielo manderemmo.
5. Ce li venderà.

(*b*) Translate into Italian:

1. He will give it (*f.*) to her.
2. He would show it (*m.*) to us.
3. They will read them to me.
4. I will speak of it to them.
5. Mary wrote it (*f.*) to me.

LESSON XXIX

The Imperfect Subjunctive

To form the imperfect subjunctive add the following endings to the stem of the verb. The characteristic vowel of the infinitive is retained in all regular and many irregular verbs. The endings are:

-ssi	-ssimo
-ssi	-ste
-sse	-ssero

As a general rule the present or perfect subjunctive is used in a subordinate clause when the verb in the main clause is in the present, future or imperative. The imperfect or pluperfect subjunctive is used if the main verb is in any past tense:

e.g. Temevo che Carlo non venisse oggi.
I was afraid Charles might not come today.

Imperfect Subjunctive of the Model Verbs

PARLARE		V*E*NDERE	
parlassi	*I spoke* or *might speak*, etc.	vendessi	*I sold* or *might sell*, etc.
parlassi		vendessi	
parlasse		vendesse	
parl*a*ssimo		vend*e*ssimo	
parlaste		vendeste	
parl*a*ssero		vend*e*ssero	

FINIRE		PARTIRE	
finissi	*I finished* or *might finish*, etc.	partissi	*I left* or *might leave*, etc.
finissi		partissi	
finisse		partisse	
fin*i*ssimo		part*i*ssimo	
finiste		partiste	
fin*i*ssero		part*i*ssero	

Imperfect Subjunctive of the Auxiliaries

AVERE		*E*SSERE	
avessi	*I had* or *might have*,	fossi	*I was* or *might be*,
avessi	etc.	fossi	etc.
avesse		fosse	
av*e*ssimo		f*o*ssimo	
aveste		foste	
av*e*ssero		f*o*ssero	

NOTE.—Except for the characteristic vowel, the endings are the same for all conjugations. The characteristic vowel of the infinitive is retained in all regular and many irregular verbs:

e.g. comprassi	*from*	comprare	*to buy*
ricevessi	*from*	ric*e*vere	*to receive*
capissi	*from*	capire	*to understand*
avessi	*from*	avere	*to have*
venissi	*from*	venire	*to come*

Verbs with a contracted infinitive add the endings to the stem of the original infinitive:

e.g. dire (*contracted from* d*i*cere) dicessi
fare (*contracted from* f*a*cere) facessi

Note, however, the irregular forms of *e*ssere and the following two verbs:

DARE	STARE
dessi	stessi
dessi	stessi
desse	stesse
d*e*ssimo	st*e*ssimo
deste	steste
d*e*ssero	st*e*ssero

The imperfect subjunctive is used in a conditional clause to imply that the statement is either contrary to fact in the present or doubtful in the future:

e.g. Se avessi tempo, studierei molte lingue.
If I had time I should study many languages
(this implies that I have not time).

Se Roberto arrivasse in tempo, usciremmo insieme.
If Robert arrived in time we should go out together
(a condition doubtful in the future).

When the conditional clause refers to past time, the pluperfect of the subjunctive (formed from the imperfect subjunctive of the auxiliary plus the past participle) is used with the conditional perfect:

e.g. Se Carlo mi avesse parlato inglese, avrei capito tutto.
If Charles had spoken English to me, I should have understood everything.

More Compound Tenses

1. The pluperfect, which is formed from the imperfect of the auxiliary and the past participle of the verb conjugated:

   e.g. avevo parlato — *I had spoken*
   ero partito — *I had left*

2. The past anterior, which is formed from the past definite of the auxiliary and the past participle of the verb conjugated:

   e.g. ebbi parlato — *I had spoken*
   fui partito — *I had left*

3. The future perfect, which is formed from the future of the auxiliary and the past participle of the verb conjugated:

   e.g. avrò parlato — *I shall have spoken*
   sarò partito — *I shall have left*

4. The conditional perfect, which is formed from the conditional of the auxiliary and the past participle of the verb conjugated:

   e.g. avrei parlato — *I should have spoken*
   sarei partito — *I should have left*

NOTE.—The pluperfect and the past anterior have the same meaning; they denote what *had* happened. The past anterior is used after certain conjunctions of time in a subordinate clause, provided that the past definite has been used in the main clause.

e.g. Dopo che Roberto ebbe letto il telegramma, uscì.
After Robert had read the telegram, he went out.
Quando fu arrivato a casa, andò a letto.
When he reached home, he went to bed.
Appena *e*bbero veduto il Duomo, and*a*rono alla Galleria.
As soon as they had seen the Cathedral they went to the Arcades.

Other conjunctions of time are *appena* or *appena che* (as soon as), *quando* (when), *subito dopo* (immediately after).

The future perfect and the conditional perfect are used as in English, and also to express what was probable (cf. Lesson XIV for a similar use of the future tense).

Verbs followed by Prepositions

Some verbs do *not* require a preposition in Italian, whereas they do in English:

e.g.	ascoltare	*to listen to*	aspettare	*to wait for*
	cercare	*to look for*	guardare	*to look at*

Some verbs *do* require a preposition in Italian, but not in English:

e.g.	entrare in	*to enter*	obbedire a	*to obey*
	credere a	*to believe*	ricordarsi di	*to remember*

Some verbs require one preposition in Italian and another in English:

e.g.	coprire di	*to cover with*	caricare di	*to load with*
	vivere di	*to live on*	dipendere da	*to depend on*

A number of verbs take the infinitive without any intervening preposition:

e.g.	preferire	*to prefer*	bisognare	*to be necessary*
	desiderare	*to want, desire*		

Simple and Compound Tenses of Verbs

First Conjugation

Infinitive { *Present*	parlare	*to speak*
Infinitive { *Past*	aver parlato	*to have spoken*
Gerund { *Present*	parlando	*speaking*
Gerund { *Past*	avendo parlato	*having spoken*
Past participle and verbal adjective	parlato (a) (i) (e)	*spoken*
Present	parlo, *etc.*	*I speak*, etc.
Perfect	ho parlato, *etc.*	*I have spoken*, etc.
Future	parlerò, *etc.*	*I shall speak*, etc.
Future perfect	avrò parlato, *etc.*	*I shall have spoken*, etc.
Conditional { *Present*	parlerei, *etc.*	*I would speak*, etc.
Conditional { *Perfect*	avrei parlato, *etc.*	*I would have spoken*, etc.
Imperfect	parlavo, *etc.*	*I used to speak*, etc.
Pluperfect	avevo parlato, *etc.*	*I had spoken, etc.*
Past definite	parlai, *etc.*	*I spoke*, etc.
Past anterior	ebbi parlato, *etc.*	*I had spoken*, etc.
Subjunctive { *Present*	parli, *etc.*	(*that*) *I may speak*, etc.
Subjunctive { *Perfect*	abbia parlato, *etc.*	(*that*) *I may have spoken*, etc.
Subjunctive { *Imperfect*	parlassi, *etc.*	(*that*) *I might speak*, etc.
Subjunctive { *Pluperfect*	avessi parlato, *etc.*	(*that*) *I might have spoken*, etc.
Imperative	parla, parli, *etc.*	*speak!* etc.

Second Conjugation

Infinitive { *Present*	vendere	*to sell*
Infinitive { *Past*	aver venduto	*to have sold*
Gerund { *Present*	vendendo	*selling*
Gerund { *Past*	avendo venduto	*having sold*
Past participle and verbal adjective	venduto (a) (i) (e)	*sold*
Present	vendo, *etc.*	*I sell*, etc.
Perfect	ho venduto, *etc.*	*I have sold*, etc.
Future	venderò, *etc.*	*I shall sell*, etc.
Future perfect	avrò venduto, *etc.*	*I shall have sold*, etc.
Conditional { *Present*	venderei, *etc.*	*I would sell*, etc.
Conditional { *Perfect*	avrei venduto, *etc.*	*I would have sold*, etc.
Imperfect	vendevo, *etc.*	*I used to sell*, etc.
Pluperfect	avevo venduto, *etc.*	*I had sold*, etc.
Past definite	vendei (-etti), *etc.*	*I sold*, etc.
Past anterior	ebbi venduto, *etc.*	*I had sold*, etc.

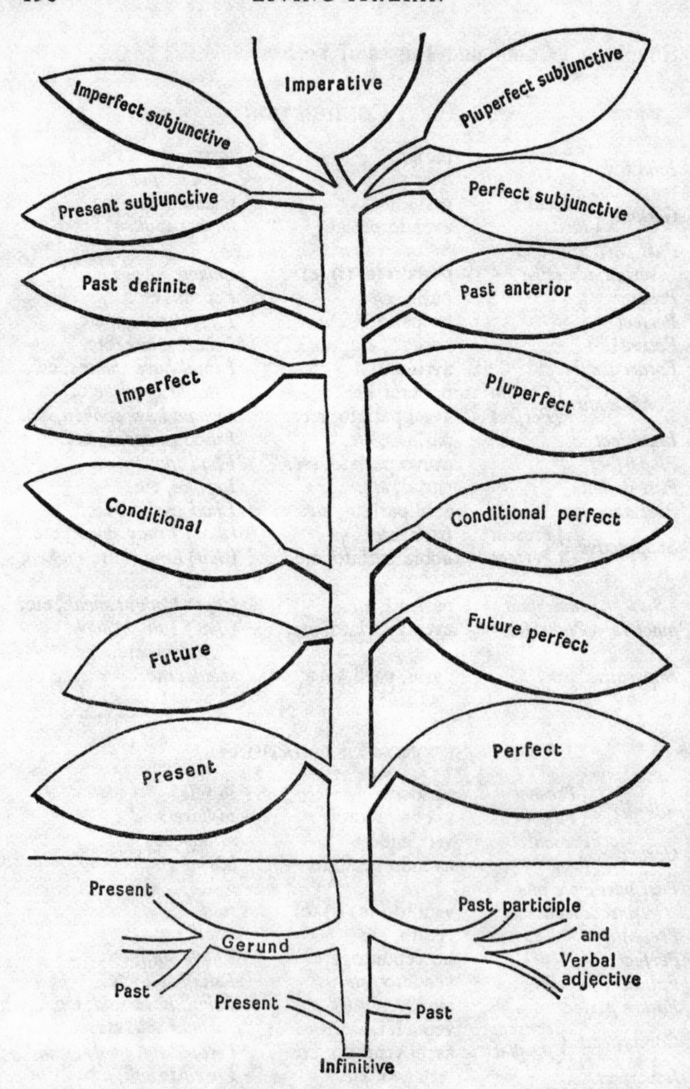

The **Verb Tree** and the table of verb tenses will help students to see, at a glance, the simple and compound tenses of verbs.

Subjunctive { *Present*	venda, *etc.*	(*that*) *I may sell*, etc.
Subjunctive { *Perfect*	*a*bbia venduto, *etc.*	(*that*) *I may have sold*, etc.
Subjunctive { *Imperfect*	vendessi, *etc.*	(*that*) *I might sell*, etc.
Subjunctive { *Pluperfect*	avessi venduto, *etc.*	(*that*) *I might have sold*, etc.
Imperative	vendi, venda, *etc.*	*sell!* etc.

THIRD CONJUGATION

Infinitive { *Present*	partire	*to leave* (*depart*)
Infinitive { *Past*	*e*ssere partito	*to have left*
Gerund { *Present*	partendo	*leaving*
Gerund { *Past*	essendo partito	*having left*
Past participle and verbal adjective	partito (a) (i) (e)	*left*
Present	parto, *etc.*	*I leave*, etc.
Perfect	sono partito (a), *etc.*	*I have left*, etc.
Future	partirò, *etc.*	*I shall leave*, etc.
Future perfect	sarò partito (a), *etc.*	*I shall have left*, etc.
Conditional { *Present*	partirei, *etc.*	*I would leave*, etc.
Conditional { *Perfect*	sarei partito (a), *etc.*	*I would have left*, etc.
Imperfect	partivo, *etc.*	*I used to leave*, etc.
Pluperfect	ero partito (a), *etc.*	*I had left*, etc.
Past definite	partii, *etc.*	*I left*, etc.
Past anterior	fui partito (a), *etc.*	*I had left*, etc.
Subjunctive { *Present*	parta, *etc.*	(*that*) *I may leave*, etc.
Subjunctive { *Perfect*	sia partito (a), *etc.*	(*that*) *I may have left*, etc.
Subjunctive { *Imperfect*	partissi, *etc.*	(*that*) *I might leave*, etc.
Subjunctive { *Pluperfect*	fossi partito (a), *etc.*	(*that*) *I might have left*, etc.
Imperative	parti, parta, *etc.*	*leave!* etc.

VOCABULARY

la fine	end	il canale	canal
la tappa	stage, halting place	il Canal Grande	Grand Canal
l'impressione	impression	il Ponte dei Sospiri	Bridge of Sighs
la g*o*ndola	gondola	il Ponte di Rialto	Rialto Bridge
il gondoliere	gondolier	l'ind*u*stria	industry
la barca a motore	motor-launch	il vetro	glass
l'isoletta	little island	la Barca Musicale	Music Boat
il modo	way, manner		

il ritorno	return	bizantino	Byzantine
il recordo	remembrance	entusi*a*stico	enthusiastic
San Marco	Saint Mark	forse	perhaps
il Palazzo Ducale	Ducal Palace	chi sa?	who knows?
		ammirare	to admire
il sogno	dream	camminare	to walk
la bellezza	beauty	scivolare	to glide, slip
la Regina dell' Adri*a*tico	Queen of the Adriatic	mancare	to fail, miss
		strano	strange

VEN*E*ZIA

Giovanni. Siamo quasi alla fine del nostro vi*a*ggio. Ven*e*zia sarà l'*u*ltima tappa.

Mario. Che bella vacanza è stata per me!

Giovanni. Avrà una strana impressione quando arriverà alla stazione di Ven*e*zia.

Mario. Perchè?

Giovanni. Perchè uscendo dalla stazione vedrà le g*o*ndole, le barche a motore, ed i pir*o*scafi che porteranno i viaggiatori agli alberghi.

Mario. Oh—come sarà interessante!

Giovanni. Durante la mia *u*ltima visita a Ven*e*zia feci quasi tutta questa città a piedi.

Mario. A piedi, ma come?

Giovanni. Lei sa che Ven*e*zia è costruita su numerose isolette che sono unite da p*i*ccoli ponti. In questo modo si può camminare da una parte all'altra, ammirando allo stesso tempo tante belle cose . . . ma *e*ccoci arrivati!

Mario. Oh—quanti gondolieri! Prenderemo anche noi una gondola?

Giovanni. Sì, ci sarà quella del nostro albergo, *e*ccola!

Mario (*entusiastico di tutto esclama*). Come sc*i*volano in silenzio sull'*a*cqua!

Giovanni. Fra poco vedrà il Ponte di Rialto, *e*ccolo!

Mario. Com'è bello!

Giovanni. Vede, ora, laggiù la Piazza San Marco?

Mario. Di che stile è la Cattedrale?

Giovanni. Bizantino. Vede il gran campanile e il Ponte dei Sospiri? (*Arrivano alla porta dell'albergo.*)

Mario. Ha ragione, tutto mi pare tanto strano. Ven*e*zia è veramente la Regina dell'Adri*a*tico!

Giovanni. Questo non è niente, domani vedrà il Palazzo Ducale, poi un altro giorno andremo all'*i*sola di Murano, famosa per l'ind*u*stria veneziana del vetro, ed una sera andremo sul Canal Grande e sentirà la m*u*sica dalla *Barca Musicale*.

Mario. Non so cosa dire, tutto mi pare un sogno!

Giovanni. Un altr'anno dovrà ritornare in It*a*lia per visitare altre città, perchè ognuna ha le sue bellezze.

Mario. Non mancherò di farlo. Quest'inverno leggerò alcuni libri sull'It*a*lia e cercherò di studiare m*e*glio la l*i*ngua. Chi sa, forse anch'io potrò aiutare qualcuno come Lei ha fatto con me quest'anno.

(*Dopo la loro visita a Venezia ritornano a Milano. Alle ore diciassette e trenta prendono il treno per Calais.*)

(*Fine*)

EXERCISES

A. Answer the following:

1. Quale impressione avrà M*a*rio quando arriverà a Ven*e*zia?
2. Perchè?
3. Come visitò una volta questa città, Giovanni?
4. Com'è costruita Ven*e*zia?
5. Che v*i*dero dal Canal Grande?
6. Di che stile è San Marco?
7. Quali sono i due ponti famosi?
8. Perchè visiteranno l'*i*sola di Murano?
9. Visiterà Ven*e*zia un giorno, Lei?
10. Quali altre città d'It*a*lia visiterà?

B. Translate:

1. At Robert's house.
2. It depends on him.
3. Looking at the bridge.
4. Looking for the hotel.
5. Living in the town.

C. (*a*) Put into the future, and

(*b*) Put into the future perfect:

1. Finisco il lavoro.
2. Vendiamo la m*a*cchina.
3. C*o*mprano la casa.
4. Arriva all'una.
5. Parte a mezzanotte.

D. (*a*) Translate into English:

1. Se Maria fosse arrivata prima, avrebbe trovato suo cugino a casa.
2. Se Giovanni fosse ricco, comprerebbe quell'automobile.
3. Se Roberto avesse studiato bene, suo padre sarebbe stato contento.
4. Se ricevessi una l*e*ttera, sarei felice.
5. Se and*a*ssimo a Pisa, vedremmo la Torre Pendente.

(*b*) Translate into Italian:

1. If we had enough money, we would buy a house.
2. If the ladies had arrived in time, they would have seen the race.

3. If we spoke French, the children would understand us.
4. If Mary came before midday, she would see her friend.
5. If you wrote to me in Italian, I would answer your letter.

E. Form sentences using the following words:

1. qualche volta
2. fra un anno
3. sei mesi fa
4. ieri
5. spesso
6. mai
7. prima di
8. prima che
9. appena
10. benchè

LESSON XXX

Idiomatic Expressions with certain Verbs

AVERE

aver caldo	*to be hot, warm*
aver freddo	*to be cold*
aver torto	*to be wrong*
aver ragione	*to be right*
aver appetito (fame)	*to be hungry*
aver sete	*to be thirsty*
aver luogo	*to take place*
aver sonno	*to be sleepy*
aver paura	*to be afraid*
aver bisogno di	*to be in need of*
aver appunto	*to have just*

*E*SSERE

*e*ssere in ritardo	*to be late*
*e*ssere d'accordo	*to agree*
*e*ssere sul punto di *or* *e*ssere per	*to be on the point of*
*e*ssere di	*to belong to*

ANDARE

andare a piedi	*to walk*
andare in carrozza	*to ride in a carriage*
andare in autom*o*bile *or* in m*a*cchina	*to ride in a motor car*
andare a cavallo	*to ride on horseback*
and*a*rsene	*to go away, to be off*

DARE

dare del tu	*to address familiarly*
dare in pr*e*stito	*to lend*
dare gli esami	*to take an examination*

FARE

far bel tempo	*to be fine weather*
far cattivo tempo	*to be bad weather*
far caldo	*to be warm, hot*
far freddo	*to be cold*
far *u*mido	*to be damp*
far colazione	*to have breakfast, lunch*
far finta di	*to pretend*
far piacere	*to please*
far male	*to hurt, harm*
far bene	*to do good*
fare una v*i*sita	*to pay a visit*
fare una passeggiata	*to go for a walk*
fare una domanda	*to ask a question*
fare attenzione	*to pay attention*
far capolino	*to peep (out, in)*
fare un br*i*ndisi	*to drink a toast*
far fare	*to have made*
Note also:	
non fa niente *or* nulla	*it does not matter*, or *never mind*

STARE

stare in piedi	*to stand*
stare per	*to be about to*
star zitto	*to be silent*

VOLERE

voler bene	*to be fond of*
voler dire	*to mean*

SAPERE

sapere a mente *or* a mem*o*ria	*to know by heart*

Classified Vocabulary

1. Nomi di Ragazzi	*Boys' names*	2. Nomi di Ragazze	*Girls' names*
Luigi	*Louis*	Anna	*Ann*
Lorenzo	*Lawrence*	Maria	*Mary*
Pietro	*Peter*	Caterina	*Catherine*

P*a*olo	*Paul*
Giovanni	*John*
Giuseppe	*Joseph*
Guglielmo	*William*
Ant*o*nio	*Anthony*
Leonardo	*Leonard*
Francesco	*Francis*
Ida	*Ida*
Rita	*Rita*
Ada	*Ada*
Beatrice	*Beatrice*
Lucia	*Lucy*
Isabella	*Isabel*
Elisabetta	*Elizabeth*

3. ANIMALI DOM*E*STICI	*Domestic animals*
il cane	*dog*
il gatto	*cat*
il cavallo	*horse*
il toro	*bull*
la mucca, vacca	*cow*
il bue	*ox*
l'*a*sino, il ciuco, il somaro	*ass, donkey*
il maiale	*pig*
il mulo	*mule*
il con*i*glio	*rabbit*

4. ANIMALI SELV*A*TICI	*Wild animals*
il leone	*lion*
la tigre	*tiger*
l'elefante	*elephant*
il lupo	*wolf*
la volpe	*fox*
l'orso	*bear*
la giraffa	*giraffe*
la zebra	*zebra*
il coccodrillo	*crocodile*
il gorilla	*gorilla*

5. FIORI	*Flowers*
il g*i*glio	*lily*
il gar*o*fano	*carnation*
il pap*a*vero	*poppy*
la violetta	*violet*
l'ort*e*nsia	*hydrangea*
la gl*i*cine	*wistaria*
la begonia	*begonia*
il ger*a*nio	*geranium*
la d*a*lia	*dahlia*
la f*u*csia	*fuchsia*

6. *A*LBERI	*Trees*
il cipresso	*cypress*
il castagno	*chestnut*
la quercia	*oak*
il f*a*ggio	*beech*
l'oleandro	*oleander*
la magn*o*lia	*magnolia*
il m*a*ndorlo	*almond tree*
l'olivo	*olive*
il pino	*pine*
l'abete	*fir*

7. LE FRUTTA	*Fruit*
la mela	*apple*
la pera	*pear*
l'ar*a*ncia	*orange*
la pesca	*peach*

8. UCCELLI	*Birds*
la rondinella	*swallow*
l'all*o*dola	*sky-lark*
l'usignolo	*nightingale*
il merlo	*blackbird*

il melone (popone)	*melon*	il tordo	*thrush*
il cocomero	*water-melon*	il pettirosso	*robin redbreast*
il fico	*fig*	il passero	*sparrow*
la susina	*plum*	il piccione	*pigeon*
l'uva	*grape(s)*	la colomba	*dove*
l'albicocca	*apricot*	il pappagallo	*parrot*

9. ERBE	*Vegetables*	10. MESTIERI	*Trades*
i piselli	*peas*	il macellaio	*butcher*
i fagioli	*beans*	il fornaio (panettiere)	*baker*
i carciofi	*artichokes*	il lattaio	*milkman*
il pomodoro *pl.* pomidoro *or* pomodori	*tomato*	il fruttivendolo	*greengrocer, fruiterer*
il cavolo	*cabbage*	il pescivendolo	*fishmonger*
il cavolfiore	*cauliflower*	il pasticciere	*confectioner*
i fagiolini	*French beans*	il droghiere	*grocer*
le carote	*carrots*	il tabaccaio	*tobacconist*
le patate	*potatoes*	il postino	*postman*
gli zucchini	*small vegetable marrows*	il sarto	*tailor*

VOCABULARY

il disturbo	disturbance, trouble	rimanere (*irr.*)	to remain, stay
		ringraziare	to thank
il regalo	present, gift	caricare	to lade, load
la conferenza	lecture, conference	ciao	goodbye, hello (*colloq.*)
appena	scarcely, barely	perbacco!	by Jove!

IL RITORNO

Ritornato in Inghilterra, e quando è a casa da appena due giorni, Giovanni riceve la lettera seguente.

Via Trafalgar, 25,
Londra.
10 settembre 1960.

Caro Giovanni,

*E*ccomi a casa. Spero che tu *a*bbia fatto un buon vi*a*ggio fino a casa tua. Vedi, ti do del tu. Siamo buoni amici ora, non è vero? Non so come ringraziarti del disturbo che hai preso per me durante il nostro soggiorno in It*a*lia.

Non potrò mai dimenticare questa vacanza passata con te. I miei genitori sono contenti dei regali, mia sorella è molto contenta della sciarpa di seta pura, e per me ci sono le belle fotografie prese nelle v*a*rie città; saranno sempre un buon ricordo della mia v*i*sita in It*a*lia con te.

Quest'inverno riprenderò lo st*u*dio della l*i*ngua italiana e, se avrò tempo, andrò, anche, ad alcune conferenze italiane.

Spesso penso alle belle serate passate insieme, alle gite fatte intorno alle città ed ai laghi.

Ora devo m*e*ttermi al lavoro. Le vacanze sono finite e lontane, ma i ricordi rim*a*ngono sempre. Di nuovo, mille gr*a*zie di tutto.

Ciao, Giovanni; saluti ai tuoi genitori, ed a te,

il tuo amico,

M*a*rio.

EXERCISES

A. Translate:

1. Where are Isabel and Catherine?
2. I think they have gone out.
3. Have William and Lawrence returned?
4. No, not yet, they will be home at 11.30 a.m.
5. I saw four oxen and two mules yesterday.
6. We saw many donkeys laden with fruit and vegetables.
7. Where were they going?
8. To the market; we also went there and bought some fruit.
9. We bought peaches, plums, grapes and a water-melon.
10. Do you like melons? Yes, but I prefer peaches.

B. Translate:

1. A che ora fa colazione, Lei?
2. Verso l'una, di s*o*lito.
3. Oggi fa caldo, ieri faceva molto freddo.
4. Abbiamo fatto un br*i*ndisi ad alcuni amici.
5. Partiranno per l'It*a*lia fra due giorni.

C. Give the Italian for:

1. November 11th, 1945.
2. December 1st, 1958.
3. This student is twenty-two years old.
4. Two hundred years ago.
5. Five thousand nine hundred and seventy.

D. Translate the words in brackets:

1. Quando (*I was*) dieci anni, (*I spoke*) due l*i*ngue.
2. Questa città non ha (*any*) museo.
3. (*Do you know*) questi signori?
4. No, ma (*I know*) che p*a*rlano italiano.
5. Rita ha più (*than*) d*o*dici anni.

E. Conjugate in the imperfect and pluperfect tenses:

(*a*) l*e*ggere (*b*) volere (*c*) venire

F. (*a*) Find the nouns derived from the following verbs:

arrivare
ballare
cenare
domandare
entrare
fumare
girare
invitare
l*e*ggere
mostrare
nevicare
ordinare
p*e*rdere
risp*o*ndere
salire
telefonare
usare
vedere

(*b*) Find verbs from the nouns:

l'aug*u*rio
la bevanda
la celebrazione
la divisione
l'educazione
la fine
il gelo
l'indicazione
il lavoro
la misura
la nuotata
l'osservazione
la partenza
la quota
il ritorno
lo st*u*dio
la trovata
l'uscita
il vi*a*ggio

REVISION TEST

A. Translate and put into the plural:

1. That hand
2. This arm.
3. That foot.
4. The eye.
5. The ear.
6. I like fruit.
7. This town is old.
8. This grape is sweet.
9. That artist is clever.
10. That poem is long.

B. Translate:

1. Non prendevo mai l'autob*us*.
2. Non incontravamo nessuno.
3. Questi ragazzi non hanno nè padre nè madre.
4. Non starò che due settimane in It*a*lia.
5. Questa mano mi fa male.
6. Queste signorine hanno mal di testa.
7. Dove ha messo il mio biglietto?
8. Non so, sarà sul tavolino.
9. Conosco quella signora.
10. Mi sembra che sia la signora Valli.

C. Translate:

1. Travelling from Milan to Florence . . .
2. By repeating these words . . .
3. Having finished the letter . . .
4. Having been to Rome . . .
5. Saying this phrase . . .
6. Entering the station . . .

D. Translate:

1. We were speaking French.
2. I used to go to France every year.
3. They were selling their house.
4. Peter used to do his work at home.
5. They used to finish at midday.
6. Every year he would go to the same place.

E. Give the comparative and superlative of:

1. buono
2. cattivo
3. grande
4. lungo
5. ricco

F. Translate:

1. We left at midnight.
2. We arrived at 8 p.m.
3. I read this book two years ago.
4. Margaret wrote to me last week.
5. We went out together every Monday.
6. Have you been to the theatre lately?
7. No, but we will go to the opera next week.
8. I telephoned Robert two days ago.
9. Do you think he will come?
10. No, I think he has a cold.

G. Give (*a*) the third persons singular and plural, imperfect tense, of the following verbs:

1. cantare
2. ric*e*vere
3. fare
4. tradurre
5. finire

(*b*) the first persons singular and plural, past definite, of:

1. avere
2. andare
3. *e*ssere
4. partire
5. l*e*ggere

H. Give the comparative and the superlative of the following adverbs:

1. bene
2. male
3. molto
4. poco

I. Translate the following conversation:

Pietro. Ci sarà un bel programma domani alla r*a*dio.
Paolo. A che ora?
Pietro. Alle ventitrè.
Paolo. Così tardi? Sono tanto stanco a quell'ora dopo il mio lavoro.
Pietro. Ma quando saprai chi suonerà il violino e chi

canterà sono sicuro che non vorrai mancare questo programma.

Paolo. Dimmi, chi saranno gli artisti?

Pietro. Guarda nel Radiocorriere e troverai i loro nomi.

Paolo. Non ho tempo di guardare adesso, dimmi tu.

Pietro. Il famoso violinista, Raimondo Pucci.

Paolo. Perbacco, hai ragione, non vorrò mancarlo, e chi canterà?

Pietro. La Celli.

Paolo. Che bel programma!

J. Translate:

Many years ago my father bought a house in the country. My parents, my little sister and I used to spend our summer holidays there every year. Sometimes we invited friends, and we used to go out together for the whole day. The fresh air and the outdoor life did us so much good.

K. Answer the following questions on grammar rules:

1. When is the definite article used in Italian and not in English?
2. When is the indefinite article omitted in Italian and not in English?
3. With what does the past participle of a compound tense agree?
4. Translate "some" in three different ways.
5. Translate "only" in three ways.
6. How do masculine nouns ending in *-a* form their plural? Give an example.
7. How do nouns ending in *-ista* form their plural? Give two examples.
8. Give the different forms of *bello*, with examples.
9. Give the different forms of *buono*, with examples.
10. Name two nouns ending in *-o* which have a feminine plural in *-a*.
11. How are adverbs formed? Give examples.
12. How are the comparatives and superlatives of adjectives formed in Italian?

13. When is "than" translated by *di*?
14. When is "than" translated by *che*? Give two or three examples.
15. Explain the orthographic changes of verbs ending in *-care* and *-gare*.
16. Give the comparative and superlative of the irregular adverbs *bene* and *male*.
17. What is an impersonal verb? Name two or three.
18. Name two suffixes.
19. Name two prefixes.
20. Name two idiomatic uses of the preposition *da*.

APPENDICES

1. CONJUGATION OF THE AUXILIAR

Infinitive	*Gerund and Past Participle*	*Present Indicative*	*Future*	*Conditional*
AVERE *to have*	avendo avuto	ho hai ha abbiamo avete hanno	avrò avrai avrà avremo avrete avranno	avrei avresti avrebbe avremmo avreste avrebbero
ESSERE *to be*	essendo stato	sono sei è siamo siete sono	sarò sarai sarà saremo sarete saranno	sarei saresti sarebbe saremmo sareste sarebbero

2. CONJUGATION OF TH

Infinitive	*Gerund and Past Participle*	*Present Indicative*	*Future*	*Conditional*
PARLARE *to speak*	parlando parlato	parlo parli parla parliamo parlate parlano	parlerò parlerai parlerà parleremo parlerete parleranno	parlerei parleresti parlerebbe parleremmo parlereste parlerebbero
VENDERE *to sell*	vendendo venduto	vendo vendi vende vendiamo vendete vendono	venderò venderai venderà venderemo venderete venderanno	venderei venderesti venderebbe venderemmo vendereste venderebbero
CAPIRE *to understand*	capendo capito	capisco capisci capisce capiamo capite capiscono	capirò capirai capirà capiremo capirete capiranno	capirei capiresti capirebbe capiremmo capireste capirebbero
PARTIRE *to depart*	partendo partito	parto parti *etc.*	partirò partirai *etc.*	partirei partiresti *etc.*

RBS *AVERE* AND *ESSERE*

rfect	Past Definite	Present Subjunctive	Imperfect Subjunctive	Imperative	Present Perfect
o	ebbi	*a*bbia	avessi	—	ho avuto
i	avesti	*a*bbia	avessi	abbi	*etc.*
a	ebbe	*a*bbia	avesse	*a*bbia	
amo	avemmo	abbiamo	av*e*ssimo	abbiamo	
ate	aveste	abbiate	aveste	abbiate	
ano	*e*bbero	*a*bbiano	av*e*ssero	*a*bbiano	
	fui	sia	fossi	—	sono stato (a)
	fosti	sia	fossi	sii	*etc.*
	fu	sia	fosse	sia	
amo	fummo	siamo	f*o*ssimo	siamo	
ate	foste	siate	foste	siate	
o	f*u*rono	s*i*ano	f*o*ssero	s*i*ano	

ODEL REGULAR VERBS

rfect	Past Definite	Present Subjunctive	Imperfect Subjunctive	Imperative	Present Perfect
vo	parlai	parli	parlassi	—	ho parlato
avi	parlasti	parli	parlassi	parla	*etc.*
va	parlò	parli	parlasse	parli	
avamo	parlammo	parliamo	parl*a*ssimo	parliamo	
avate	parlaste	parliate	parlaste	parlate	
avano	parl*a*rono	p*a*rlino	parl*a*ssero	p*a*rlino	
evo	vendei(-etti)	venda	vendessi	—	ho venduto
evi	vendesti	venda	vendessi	vendi	*etc.*
eva	vendè(-ette)	venda	vendesse	venda	
evamo	vendemmo	vendiamo	vend*e*ssimo	vendiamo	
evate	vendeste	vendiate	vendeste	vendete	
evano	vend*e*rono (-*e*ttero)	v*e*ndano	vend*e*ssero	v*e*ndano	
o	capii	capisca	capissi	—	ho capito
i	capisti	capisca	capissi	capisci	*etc.*
a	capì	capisca	capisse	capisca	
amo	capimmo	capiamo	cap*i*ssimo	capiamo	
ate	capiste	capiate	capiste	capite	
ano	cap*i*rono	cap*i*scano	cap*i*ssero	cap*i*scano	
vo	partii	parta	partissi	—	sono partito (a)
vi	partisti	parta	partissi	parti	*etc.*
.	*etc.*	*etc.*	*etc.*	parta *etc.*	

Here, in alphabetical order, are the most important Irregular Ver
conjugated according to the rules given for the model verbs.
The rule for forming the Past Definite of Irregular Verbs is gi

Infinitive	*Gerund and Past Participle*	*Present Indicative*	*Future*	*Conditional*
ANDARE *to go*	andando andato	vado vai va andiamo andate vanno	andrò andrai *etc.*	andrei andresti *etc.*
APRIRE *to open*	aprendo aperto	apro apri *etc.*	aprirò aprirai *etc.*	aprirei apriresti *etc.*
BERE *to drink* (*contracted from* bevere)	bevendo bevuto	bevo bevi *etc.*	berrò berrai *etc.*	berrei berresti *etc.*
CADERE *to fall*	cadendo caduto	cado cadi *etc.*	cadrò cadrai *etc.*	cadrei cadresti *etc.*
CHI*e*DERE *to ask*	chiedendo chiesto	chiedo chiedi *etc.*	chiederò chiederai *etc.*	chiederei chiederesti *etc.*
CHI*u*DERE *to close, shut*	chiudendo chiuso	chiudo chiudi *etc.*	chiuderò chiuderai *etc.*	chiuderei chiuderesti *etc.*
CONOSCERE *to know*	conoscendo conosciuto	conosco conosci *etc.*	conoscerò conoscerai *etc.*	conoscerei conoscerestei *etc.*
CONTENERE *to contain*	*see* tenere			
COPRIRE *to cover*	*see* aprire			
C*o*RRERE *to run*	correndo corso	corro corri *etc.*	correrò correrai *etc.*	correrei correresti *etc.*
CR*e*SCERE *to grow*	crescendo cresciuto	cresco cresci *etc.*	crescerò crescerai *etc.*	crescerei cresceresti *etc.*
DARE *to give*	dando dato	do dai dà diamo date danno	darò darai *etc.*	darei daresti *etc.*
DEC*i*DERE *to decide*	decidendo deciso	decido decidi *etc.*	deciderò deciderai *etc.*	deciderei decideresti *etc.*

RBS

ly the first two persons of Regular Tenses are given; the others are

Lesson XXV.

rfect	*Past Definite*	*Present Subjunctive*	*Imperfect Subjunctive*	*Imperative*	*Present Perfect*
vo vi :.	andai andasti *etc.*	vada vada vada andiamo andiate v*a*dano	andassi andassi *etc.*	— va' vada andiamo andate v*a*dano	sono andato (a) *etc.*
'o i .	aprii apristi *etc.*	apra apra *etc.*	aprissi aprissi *etc.*	— apri apra *etc.*	ho aperto *etc.*
vo vi :.	bevvi *or* bevetti bevesti *etc.*	beva beva *etc.*	bevessi bevessi *etc.*	— bevi beva *etc.*	ho bevuto *etc.*
vo vi .	caddi cadesti *etc.*	cada cada *etc.*	cadessi cadessi *etc.*	— cadi cada *etc.*	sono caduto (a) *etc.*
levo levi .	chiesi chiedesti *etc.*	chieda chieda *etc.*	chiedessi chiedessi *etc.*	— chiedi chieda *etc.*	ho chiesto *etc.*
levo levi .	chiusi chiudesti *etc.*	chiuda chiuda *etc.*	chiudessi chiudessi *etc.*	— chiudi chiuda *etc.*	ho chiuso *etc.*
scevo scevi .	conobbi conoscesti *etc.*	conosca conosca *etc.*	conoscessi conoscessi *etc.*	— conosci conosca *etc.*	ho conosciuto *etc.*
vo vi .	corsi corresti *etc.*	corra corra *etc.*	corressi corressi *etc.*	— corri corra *etc.*	ho corso *etc.*
evo evi .	crebbi crescesti *etc.*	cresca cresca *etc.*	crescessi crescessi *etc.*	— cresci cresca	sono } cresciuto ho } *etc.*
  .	diedi *or* detti desti diede *or* dette demmo deste di*e*dero	dia dia *etc.*	dessi dessi *etc.*	— da' dia *etc.*	ho dato *etc.*
levo levi .	decisi decidesti *etc.*	decida decida *etc.*	decidessi decidessi *etc.*	— decidi decida *etc.*	ho deciso *etc.*

Infinitive	*Gerund and Past Participle*	*Present Indicative*	*Future*	*Conditional*
DIRE *to say, tell* (*contracted from* dicere)	dicendo detto	dico dici dice diciamo dite d*i*cono	dirò dirai *etc.*	direi diresti *etc.*
DIVENIRE *to become*	*see* venire			
DOVERE *to have to, to be obliged to, to owe*	dovendo dovuto	devo devi deve dobbiamo dovete d*e*vono	dovrò dovrai *etc.*	dovrei dovresti *etc.*
FARE *to do, make* (*contracted from* facere)	facendo fatto	faccio fai fa facciamo fate fanno	farò farai *etc.*	farei faresti *etc.*
GI*U*NGERE *to arrive, reach*	giungendo giunto	giungo giungi *etc.*	giungerò giungerai *etc.*	giungerei giungeresti *etc.*
L*E*GGERE *to read*	leggendo letto	leggo leggi *etc.*	leggerò leggerai *etc.*	leggerei leggeresti *etc.*
M*E*TTERE *to put*	mettendo messo	metto metti *etc.*	metterò metterai *etc.*	metterei metteresti *etc.*
MORIRE *to die*	morendo morto	mu*o*io muori muore moriamo morite mu*o*iono	morirò *or* morrò morirai *etc.*	morirei moriresti *etc.*
N*A*SCERE *to be born*	nascendo nato	nasco nasci *etc.*	nascerò nascerai *etc.*	nascerei nasceresti *etc.*
NASC*O*NDERE *to hide, conceal*	nascondendo nascosto	nascondo nascondi *etc.*	nasconderò nasconderai *etc.*	nasconderei nasconderest *etc.*
OFFRIRE *to offer*	*see* aprire			
P*E*RDERE *to lose*	perdendo perso *or* perduto	perdo perdi *etc.*	perderò perderai *etc.*	perderei perderesti *etc.*
PERM*E*TTERE *to allow, permit*	*see* mettere			
PIACERE *to please*	piacendo piaciuto	piaccio piaci piace piacciamo piacete pi*a*cciono	piacerò piacerai *etc.*	piacerei piaceresti *etc.*

...rfect	*Past Definite*	*Present Subjunctive*	*Imperfect Subjunctive*	*Imperative*	*Present Perfect*
...o ...i ...	dissi dicesti *etc.*	dica dica *etc.*	dicessi dicessi *etc.*	— di' dica *etc.*	ho detto *etc.*
...vo ...vi ...	dovei *or* dovetti dovesti *etc.*	debba debba debba dobbiano dobbiate d*e*bbano	dovessi dovessi *etc.*	*No imperative*	ho dovuto *etc.*
...o ...i ...	feci facesti fece facemmo faceste f*e*cero	faccia faccia *etc.*	facessi facessi *etc.*	— fa' faccia *etc.*	ho fatto *etc.*
...gevo ...gevi ...	giunsi giungesti *etc.*	giunga giunga *etc.*	giungessi giungessi *etc.*	— giungi giunga *etc.*	sono giunto (a) *etc.*
...vo ...vi ...	lessi leggesti *etc.*	legga legga *etc.*	leggessi leggessi *etc.*	— leggi legga *etc.*	ho letto *etc.*
...evo ...evi ...	misi mettesti *etc.*	metta metta *etc.*	mettessi mettessi *etc.*	— metti metta *etc.*	ho messo *etc.*
...vo ...vi ...	morii moristi *etc.*	mu*o*ia mu*o*ia mu*o*ia moriamo moriate mu*o*iano	morissi morissi *etc.*	— muori mu*o*ia *etc.*	sono morto (a) *etc.*
...evo ...evi ...	n*a*cqui nascesti *etc.*	nasca nasca *etc.*	nascessi nascessi *etc.*	— nasci nasca *etc.*	sono nato (a) *etc.*
...ondevo ...ondevi ...c.	nascosi nascondesti *etc.*	nasconda nasconda *etc.*	nascondessi nascondessi *etc.*	— nascondi nasconda *etc.*	ho nascosto *etc.*
...evo ...evi ...c.	persi perdesti *etc.*	perda perda *etc.*	perdessi perdessi *etc.*	— perdi perda *etc.*	ho perso *or* perduto *etc.*
...evo ...evi ...c.	piacqui piacesti *etc.*	piaccia piaccia *etc.*	piacessi piacessi *etc.*	— piaci piaccia *etc.*	ho piaciuto *etc.*

Infinitive	Gerund and Past Participle	Present Indicative	Future	Conditional
PIOVERE *to rain*	piovendo piovuto	piove	pioverà	pioverebbe
POTERE *to be able*	potendo potuto	posso puoi può possiamo potete possono	potrò potrai *etc.*	potrei potresti *etc.*
PRENDERE *to take*	prendendo preso	prendo prendi *etc.*	prenderò prenderai *etc.*	prenderei prenderesti *etc.*
RICONOSCERE *to recognise*	*see* conoscere			
RIDERE *to laugh*	ridendo riso	rido ridi *etc.*	riderò riderai *etc.*	riderei rideresti *etc.*
RIMANERE *to remain*	rimanendo rimasto	rimango rimani rimane rimaniamo rimanete rimangono	rimarrò rimarrai *etc.*	rimarrei rimarresti *etc.*
RISPONDERE *to reply*	rispondendo risposto	rispondo rispondi *etc.*	risponderò risponderai *etc.*	risponderei risponderesti *etc.*
RIUSCIRE *to succeed*	*see* uscire			
SALIRE *to mount, ascend*	salendo salito	salgo sali sale saliamo salite salgono	salirò salirai *etc.*	salirei saliresti *etc.*
SAPERE *to know*	sapendo saputo	so sai sa sappiamo sapete sanno	saprò saprai *etc.*	saprei sapresti *etc.*
SCEGLIERE *to choose*	scegliendo scelto	scelgo scegli sceglie scegliamo scegliete scelgono	sceglierò sceglierai *etc.*	sceglierei sceglieresti *etc.*
SCENDERE *to descend*	scendendo sceso	scendo scendi *etc.*	scenderò scenderai *etc.*	scenderei scenderesti *etc.*
SCOMMETTERE *to bet, wager*	*see* mettere			
SCOPRIRE *to discover*	*see* aprire			
SCRIVERE *to write*	scrivendo scritto	scrivo scrivi *etc.*	scriverò scriverai *etc.*	scriverei scriveresti *etc.*

erfect	Past Definite	Present Subjunctive	Imperfect Subjunctive	Imperative	Present Perfect
veva	piovve	piova	piovesse	*No imperative*	ha è } piovuto
evo evi tc.	potei potesti *etc.*	possa possa *etc.*	potessi potessi *etc.*	*No imperative*	ho potuto *etc.*
ndevo ndevi tc.	presi prendesti *etc.*	prenda prenda *etc.*	prendessi prendessi *etc.*	— prendi prenda *etc.*	ho preso *etc.*
evo evi tc.	risi ridesti *etc.*	rida rida *etc.*	ridessi ridessi *etc.*	— ridi *etc.*	ho riso *etc.*
anevo anevi tc.	rimasi rimanesti *etc.*	rimanga rimanga *etc.*	rimanessi rimanessi *etc.*	— rimani rimanga *etc.*	sono rimasto (a) *etc.*
ondevo ondevi tc.	risposi rispondesti *etc.*	risponda risponda *etc.*	rispondessi rispondessi *etc.*	— rispondi risponda *etc.*	ho risposto *etc.*
vo vi tc.	salii salisti *etc.*	salga salga *etc.*	salissi salissi *etc.*	— sali salga *etc.*	sono salito (a) *etc.*
evo evi tc.	seppi sapesti *etc.*	s*a*ppia s*a*ppia *etc.*	sapessi sapessi *etc.*	— sappi s*a*ppia *etc.*	ho saputo *etc.*
glievo glievi tc.	scelsi scegliesti *etc.*	scelga scelga *etc.*	scegliessi scegliessi *etc.*	— scegli scelga *etc.*	ho scelto *etc.*
ndevo ndevi tc.	scesi scendesti *etc.*	scenda scenda *etc.*	scendessi scendessi *etc.*	— scendi scenda *etc.*	sono sceso (a) *etc.*
vevo vevi tc.	scrissi scrivesti *etc.*	scriva scriva *etc.*	scrivessi scrivessi *etc.*	— scrivi scriva *etc.*	ho scritto *etc.*

Infinitive	*Gerund and Past Participle*	*Present Indicative*	*Future*	*Conditional*
SEDERE	sedendo	siedo *or* seggo	sederò	sederei
to sit	seduto	siedi	sederai	sederesti
		siede	*etc.*	*etc.*
SEDERSI		sediamo		
to sit down		sedete		
		s*ie*dono		
		or seggono		
SOFFRIRE	*see* aprire			
to suffer				
SORR*i*DERE	*see* ridere			
to smile				
SP*e*NDERE	*see* prendere			
to spend				
SP*i*NGERE	spingendo	spingo	spingerò	spingerei
to push	spinto	spingi	spingerai	spingeresti
		etc.	*etc.*	*etc.*
STARE	stando	sto	starò	starei
to stay (*be*)	stato	stai	starai	staresti
		sta	*etc.*	*etc.*
		stiamo		
		state		
		stanno		
TENERE	tenendo	tengo	terrò	terrei
to hold	tenuto	tieni	terrai	terresti
		tiene	*etc.*	*etc.*
		teniamo		
		tenete		
		t*e*ngono		
TOGLIERE	togliendo	tolgo	toglierò	toglierei
to take off	tolto	togli	toglierai	toglieresti
		toglie	*etc.*	*etc.*
		togliamo		
		togliete		
		t*o*lgono		
TRADURRE	traducendo	traduco	tradurrò	tradurrei
to translate (*contracted from* traducere)	tradotto	traduci	tradurrai	tradurresti
		etc.	*etc.*	*etc.*
UDIRE	udendo	odo	udirò	udirei
to hear	udito	odi	udirai	udiresti
		ode	*etc.*	*etc.*
		udiamo		
		udite		
		*o*dono		
USCIRE	uscendo	esco	uscirò	uscirei
to go out	uscito	esci	uscirai	usciresti
		esce	*etc.*	*etc.*
		usciamo		
		uscite		
		*e*scono		

rfect	Past Definite	Present Subjunctive	Imperfect Subjunctive	Imperative	Present Perfect
vo	sedei	sieda *or* segga	sedessi	—	sono seduto (a)
vi	sedesti	segga	sedessi	siedi	*etc.*
.	*etc.*	*etc.*	*etc.*	segga	
				etc.	
gevo	spinsi	spinga	spingessi	—	ho spinto
gevi	spingesti	spinga	spingessi	spingi	*etc.*
:.	*etc.*	*etc.*	*etc.*	spinga	
				etc.	
	stetti	stia	stessi	—	sono stato (a)
	stesti	stia	stessi	sta'	*etc.*
:.	stette	stia	*etc.*	stia	
	stemmo	stiamo		*etc.*	
	steste	stiate			
	st*e*ttero	st*i*ano			
vo	tenni	tenga	tenessi	—	ho tenuto
vi	tenesti	tenga	tenessi	tieni	*etc.*
:.	*etc.*	*etc.*	*etc.*	tenga	
				etc.	
evo	tolsi	tolga	togliessi	—	ho tolto
evi	togliesti	tolga	togliessi	togli	*etc.*
:.	*etc.*	*etc.*	*etc.*	tolga	
				etc.	
ucevo	tradussi	traduca	traducessi	—	ho tradotto
ucevi	traducesti	traduca	traducessi	traduci	*etc.*
:.	*etc.*	*etc.*	*etc.*	traduca *etc.*	
o	udii	oda	udissi	—	ho udito
i	udisti	oda	udissi	odi	*etc.*
c.	*etc.*	*etc.*	*etc.*	oda	
				etc.	
vo	uscii	esca	uscissi	—	sono uscito (a)
vi	ŭscisti	esca	uscissi	esci	*etc.*
c.	*etc.*	*etc.*	*etc.*	esca	
				etc.	

Infinitive	*Gerund and Past Participle*	*Present Indicative*	*Future*	*Conditional*
VEDERE *to see*	vedendo veduto *or* visto	vedo vedi *etc.*	vedrò vedrai *etc.*	vedrei vedresti *etc.*
VENIRE *to come*	venendo venuto	vengo vieni viene veniamo venite vengono	verrò verrai *etc.*	verrei verresti *etc.*
VOLERE *to want*	volendo voluto	voglio vuoi vuole vogliamo volete vogliono	vorrò vorrai *etc.*	vorrei vorresti *etc.*

erfect	*Past Definite*	*Present Subjunctive*	*Imperfect Subjunctive*	*Imperative*	*Present Perfect*
vo	vidi	veda	vedessi	—	ho veduto
vi	vedesti	veda	vedessi	vedi	*etc.*
c.	*etc.*	*etc.*	*etc.*	veda	
				etc.	
vo	venni	venga	venissi	—	sono venuto (a)
vi	venisti	venga	venissi	vieni	*etc.*
c.	*etc.*	*etc.*	*etc.*	venga	
				etc.	
vo	volli	voglia	volessi	—	ho voluto
vi	volesti	voglia	volessi	vogli	*etc.*
c.	*etc.*	*etc.*	*etc.*	voglia	
				etc.	

VOCABULARIES

ITALIAN-ENGLISH VOCABULARY

A

a, ad, to, at, in
abbacchio, young lamb
abbronzato, sunburnt, tanned
abitante (*m.*), inhabitant
abitare, to live, dwell
abito, dress, coat, clothes
aceto, vinegar
acqua, water
Adriatico, Adriatic
aeroplano, aeroplane
affittare, to let, hire, lease
agitato, agitated, troubled
  mare agitato, rough sea
agnello, lamb
agosto, August
aiutare, to help
albergo, hotel
albero, tree
albicocca, apricot
albicocco, apricot tree
alcuno, some, any
alfabeto, alphabet
allora, then
Alpi (*f. pl.*), Alps
alto, high, tall
altrimenti, otherwise
altro, other
alunno, pupil
alzare, to raise, lift
alzarsi, to get up
amare, to love
amaro, bitter
amica (*pl.* **amiche**) friend
amico (*pl.* **amici**), friend
ammalato, sick, unwell
ammirare, to admire
amore (*m.*), love
anche, also, too, even
ancora, still, again, yet
andare (*irr.*), to go
Andrea, Andrew
anello, ring
anglicano, Anglican
angolo, corner
animale (*m.*), animal
anitra, duck
Anna, Ann, Anne
anno, year
anno bisestile, Leap Year
ansioso, anxious
antico, ancient
Antonio, Anthony
appetito, appetite
applicare, to apply
aprile, April
aprire, to open
ara, altar
arancia, orange
aranciata, orangeade
argento, silver
aria, air
arido, dry
armadio, wardrobe, cupboard
arrivare, to arrive
arrivo, arrival
arrosto, roast
arte (*f.*), art
articolo, article
ascensore (*m.*), lift, escalator
asciugamano, towel
ascoltare, to listen
asino, donkey
aspettare, to wait
assai, quite, very
assegno, cheque
assegno turistico, tourist cheque
atrio, entrance hall, lobby
attentamente, attentively
audacia, audacity, daring
Austria, Austria
autista (*m.*), chauffeur, motor driver
automobile (*f.*), motor-car, automobile

autunno, autumn
avanti, before; forward!
avere (*irr.*), to have
azzurro, blue

B

babbo, daddy
baciare, to kiss
b*a*cio, kiss
bag*a*glio, luggage
bagno, bath
balcone (*m.*), balcony
ballare, to dance
bambino, baby
b*a*mbola, doll
banana, banana
banca, bank
Banca Commerciale, Commercial Bank
banchina, platform
banco, desk
bar (*m.*), bar
barca, boat, barge
barca a motore, motor-launch
barca a vela, sailing boat
bas*i*lica, basilica
basso, low
battistero, baptistry
bello, beautiful, fine
bene (*adv.*), well, good
benzina, petrol
bere (*irr.*), to drink
Berlino, Berlin
bevanda, drink
bianco, white
b*i*bita, drink
biblioteca, library
bicchiere (*m.*), glass, tumbler
bicicletta, bicycle
biglietto, ticket
bin*a*rio, railway line, track
biondo, fair, blonde
birra, beer
biscotto, biscuit
bistecca, beefsteak
bizantino, Byzantine
bocca, mouth
borsa, purse
bosco, wood, forest
bott*i*glia, bottle
braccialetto, bracelet
br*a*ccio, arm
bramare, to long for, yearn
brama, yearning
bravo, clever; good! splendid!
breve, brief, short
brillare, to shine
brodo, broth
bruno, (dark) brown
brutto, ugly
bue (*m.—pl.* **buoi**), ox, oxen
buono, good
burro, butter
busta, envelope
buttare, to throw

C

cabina, cabin
cadere, to fall
caffè (*m.*), coffee
caldo, hot
calend*a*rio, calendar
calmo, calm
calza, stocking
cambiare, to change
c*a*mbio, change
c*a*mera, bedroom
cameriera, maid, waitress
cameriere (*m.*), waiter
cam*i*cia, shirt
camminare, to walk
campagna, country
campana, bell
campanello, small bell
campanile (*m.*), bell tower
campo, field
canale (*m.*), canal
Canal Grande, Grand Canal
cancellare, to erase
cane (*m.*), dog
cantare, to sing
capello, hair
capire, to understand
capitale (*f.*), capital
cap*i*tolo, chapter
capo, head

capolavoro, masterpiece
capostazione (*m.*), stationmaster
cappella, chapel
cappello, hat
cappuccino, coffee (*with milk*)
caramella, boiled sweet
cardinale (*m.*), cardinal
Carlo, Charles
carne (*f.*), meat
caro, dear, expensive
carrozza, carriage
carta, paper
carta geografica, map
cartolina, postcard
casa, house
castello, castle
Caterina, Catherine
cattedrale (*f.*), cathedral
cattivo, bad, naughty
cattolico, Catholic
causa, cause
cavallo, horse
caviglia, ankle
cavolo, cabbage
celebrare, to celebrate
celebrazione (*f.*), celebration
celeste, pale blue
cena, supper
Il Cenacolo *or* **L'Ultima Cena** } The Last Supper
cenere (*f.*), ash
cento, one hundred
centrale, central
centuno, one hundred and one
cera, wax
cercare, to look for
cerino, wax match
certo, certain, sure
cestino, basket
cestino da viaggio, lunch-basket
che (*conj.*), that, than
che (*pron.*), who, whom, that, which
che cosa? what?
  ma che! of course not!
  che c'è? what is the matter?
  che peccato! what a pity!
chi, who, whom, one who . . .
chiamare, to call
chiaramente, clearly
chiave (*f.*), key
chiedere (*irr.*), to ask
chiesa, church
chiudere (*irr.*), to close
chiuso, closed
ci (*adv.*), here, there; in it
ci (*pron.*), us, to us, ourselves, to ourselves; to each other
  c'è, there is; **ci sono,** there are
ciao, goodbye, hello (*colloq.*)
ciascuno, each, each one
cibo, food
cielo, sky
ciglio, eyelash
ciliegia, cherry
cinquanta, fifty
cinquantuno, fifty-one
cinque, five
ciò, that, this
cioccolata, chocolate
cioè, namely, that is
cipolla, onion
circa, almost, about
città, town
classe (*f.*), class
clima (*m.*), climate
coccodrillo, crocodile
cocomero, watermelon
coda, queue, tail
  far coda *or* **la fila,** to form a queue
codesto, cotesto, this, that
cognato, brother-in-law
coincidenza, connection (*of trains*)
colazione (*f.*), lunch
  prima colazione, breakfast
colonna, column
collega (*m.* or *f.*), colleague
colletto, collar
collina, hill
collo, neck
colomba, dove
colore (*m.*), colour
Colosseo, Colosseum
coltello, knife
come, how, like, such as
  come sta? how are you?
cominciare, to begin

communicazione (*f.*), communication
comodo, comfortable
compleanno, birthday
completare, to complete
comprare, to buy
con, with
condire, to season
conduttore, guard
coniglio, rabbit
conoscere (*irr.*), to know (*be acquainted*)
conservare, to keep, to retain
consistere, to consist
contadino, peasant
contento, glad, satisfied
continente (*m.*), continent
continuamente, continually
conto, bill
controllo, inspection
controllore (*m.*), inspector
conversare, to converse
coperta, deck
corpo, body
corsa, race
corto, short
cosa, thing
così, so, as, thus
costa, coast
costare, to cost
costruire, to build
costume (*m.*), costume
costume da bagno, swimsuit
cotone (*m.*), cotton
cotto, cooked
cravatta, tie
credenza, sideboard
credere, to believe
croce (*f.*), cross
crudo, raw
cucchiaino, teaspoon
cucchiaio, spoon
cucina, kitchen
cucinare, to cook
cugino, cousin
cui, whom, which
cuore (*m.*), heart
cupola, dome
curiosità, curiosity

D

da, from, by
danaro, money
dappertutto, everywhere
dare (*irr.*), to give
debole, weak
decidere (*irr.*), to decide
decimo, tenth
definito, definite
del (**di** + **il**), of the
delizioso, delightful, delicious
deluso, disappointed
denaro, money
dente (*m.*), tooth
dentro, inside
destro, a destra, right, to the right
dettare, to dictate
dettato, dictation
devotissimo, *abb.* **devmo**, (yours) truly, faithfully
di, of
dicembre, December
diciannove, nineteen
diciassette, seventeen
diciotto, eighteen
dieci, ten
dietro, behind
differente, different
difficile, difficult
dimenticare, to forget
dire (*irr.*), to say
direzione (*f.*), direction
distante, distant
distanza, distance
distinti saluti, kind regards
dito (*f. pl.* **dita**), finger
diventare, to become
divertirsi, to amuse oneself
dividere (*irr.*), to divide
dizionario, dictionary
dodici, twelve
dogana, customs
doganiere (*m.*), customs officer
dolce, sweet
domanda, question
domandare, to ask

pomani, tomorrow
domenica, Sunday
domestica, servant, maid
donna, woman
dopo, after
dormire, to sleep
dove, where
due, two
dunque, then, therefore
duomo, cathedral
durare, to last

E

e, ed, and
è, is
eccetera, etcetera
eccitato, excited
ecco, here is/are, there is/are
edificare, to build
edificio (*pl.* **edifici**), building
egli, he
elegante, elegant
elettrico, electric
Elisabetta, Elizabeth
ella, she
Enrico, Henry
entrare, to enter
entrata, entrance
Epifania, Befana, Epiphany
epoca, epoch, era
erba, grass, vegetable
esagerato, exaggerated
esempio, example
espresso, express
  (caffè) espresso, strong black coffee
essa, she, it
essere (*irr.*), to be
esso, he, it
est (*m.*), east
estate (*f.*), summer (*noun*)
esterno, exterior
estero, foreign
estivo, summer (*adj.*)
età, age
eterno, eternal
Europa, Europe
evitare, to avoid

F

fabbrica, factory
facchino, porter
faccia, face
facciata, façade, front
facile, easy
fagiolino, French bean
famiglia, family
fantastico, fantastic
fantino, jockey
fare (*irr.*), to make, to do
farfalla, butterfly
farmacia, chemist's shop
farmacista (*m.* or *f.*), chemist
fatto (*noun*), fact
fatto, *p.p. of* **fare,** done, made
favore (*m.*), favour, kindness
  per favore, please
fazzoletto, handkerchief
febbraio, February
fermare, to stop
fermarsi, to stop oneself
ferrovia, railway
fertile, fertile
festa, feast
fiasco, flask
figlio, son
fila, queue, line
finale, final
fine (*f.*), end
finestra, window
finestrino, small window; carriage window
finire, to finish
fino, fine, thin
fino a, until, as far as
fiore (*m.*), flower
Firenze, Florence
fiume (*m.*), river
foglia, leaf
foglio, sheet of paper
fontana, fountain
forchetta, fork
formaggio, cheese
foro, Forum
forse, perhaps
forte, strong
fotografia, photograph

fra, between, in
fr*a*gola, strawberry
Francesco, Francis
francese, French
Fr*a*ncia, France
francobollo, stamp
frase (*f.*), phrase, sentence
fratellino, little brother
fratello, brother
freddo, cold
fresco, cool, fresh
frittata, omelet
fritto, fried
fronte (*f.*), forehead
frutta, fruit
fruttiv*e*ndolo, fruiterer
fumare, to smoke
fuoco (*pl.* **fuochi**), fire
fuori, outside
futuro, future

G

g*a*io, gay
gamba, leg
galleria, gallery, arcade, tunnel
gallina, hen
gallo, cock
gar*o*fano, carnation
gatto, cat
gelato, ice-cream
generale, general
g*e*nero, son-in-law
generosità, generosity
genitore (*m.*), father, (*pl.*) parents
genn*a*io, January
G*e*nova, Genoa
gente (*f.*), people
gentile, gentle, kind
Germ*a*nia, Germany
gesso, chalk
ghi*a*ccio, ice
già, already
giacca, jacket
Gi*a*como, James
giallo, yellow
giardino, garden
g*i*glio, lily
gin*o*cchio, knee
giocare, to play (*a game*)
gioielliere (*m.*), jeweller
gioiello, jewel
Gi*o*rgio, George
giornal*a*io, newsagent
giornale (*m.*), newspaper
giorno, day
  buon giorno, good day
gi*o*vane, young
Giovanni, John
giovanotto, youth
giovedì (*m.*), Thursday
girare, to tour
giro, tour
gita, excursion
giugno, June
Giuseppe, Joseph
giusto, just
gli, the (*def. art. m. pl.*); to him (*pron.*)
glielo, gliela, it to him, it to her
glieli, gliele, them to him, them to her
gnocco, dumpling
godere, to enjoy
gola, throat
g*o*mito, elbow
g*o*ndola, gondola
gondoliere (*m.*), gondolier
g*o*tico, Gothic
gradito, welcome
gramm*a*tica, grammar
grande, great, large, big
gr*a*zia, favour, grace
gr*a*zie, thank you
  gr*a*zie tante, many thanks
gridare, to shout
gu*a*ncia, cheek
guanciale (*m.*), pillow
guanto, glove
guardare, to look at
g*u*glia, spire
Guglielmo, William
guida, guide, guidebook
gusto, taste

I

idea, idea
ieri, yesterday
imitare, to imitate

immenso, immense
imparare, to learn
importanza, importance
impressione (*f.*), impression
in, in
incantevole, charming, enchanting
incerto, uncertain
inchiostro, ink
incitare, to incite
incitamento, incitement
incontrare, to meet
indicare, to point at
indirizzo, address
industria, industry
infatti, indeed, in fact
informazione (*f.*), information
Inghilterra, England
inglese, English
ingrato, ungrateful
ingresso, entrance
insalata, salad
insegnare, to teach
insieme, together
installare, to install
intanto, meantime, meanwhile
interdetto, forbidden
interessante, interesting
interno, interior
intorno, around
inverno, winter
invitare, to invite
io, I
isola, island
Italia, Italy
italiano, Italian
itinerario, itinerary
Iugoslavia, Jugoslavia

L

la (*pron.*), she, it, you
la (*art.*), the
là (*adv.*), there
labbro (*pl.* **labbra**) (*f.*), lip
lacrima, tear
lacrimare, to cry, weep
ladro, thief
laggiù, down there
lago (*pl.* **laghi**), lake
lampada, lamp
lampone (*m.*), raspberry
lana, wool
largo, wide
lasciare, to leave
latte (*m.*), milk
latteria, dairy
lavare, to wash
lavarsi, to wash oneself
lavorare, to work
lavoro, work
leggere, to read
legna, firewood
legno, wood
legume (*m.*), vegetable
Lei, you
lei, she, her
lento, slow
lenzuolo (*pl.* **lenzuola**) (*f.*), sheet
lesso, boiled meat
lettera, letter
letteratura, literature
letto, bed
lezione (*f.*), lesson
libero, free, vacant
libro, book
Liguria, Liguria
limonata, lemonade
limone (*m.*), lemon
limpido, limpid
lineetta, dash, hyphen
lingua, tongue, language
liquore (*m.*), liquor
lira, lira sterlina, lira (*Italian money*); English pound (*sterling*)
lo (*pl.* **gli**), the
lo (*pl.* **li**), him, it
locale, local
Londra, London
lontano, distant, far
loro, they
luce (*f.*), light
luglio, July
lui, him
Luigi, Louis
luminoso, luminous, clear
luna, moon
lunedì (*m.*), Monday

lungo (*pl.* **lunghi**), long
luogo (*pl.* **luoghi**), place

M

ma, but
macchina, machine
macchina fotografica, camera
macedonia di frutta, fruit salad
macellaio, butcher
macelleria, butcher's shop
madre, mother
maestro, master, teacher
maggio, May
maggiore, major
magnifico (*pl.* **magnifici**), magnificent
maiale (*m.*), pig
malato, sick
male, badly
mandare, to send
mangiare, to eat
Manica, English Channel
mano (*f.*), hand
manzo, beef
marciapiede (*m.*), platform
marco, mark
mare (*m.*), sea
Margherita, Margaret
margheritina, daisy
Maria, Mary
marina, seashore
Mario, Marius
marito, husband
marmellata, marmalade, jam
marmo, marble
marrone, chestnut brown
martedì (*m.*), Tuesday
Martino, Martin
marzo, March
masticare, to chew
matita, pencil
mattina, morning
me, me
medicina, medicine
medico, doctor
medio, middle
medioevale, medieval
Mediterraneo, Mediterranean
meglio, better
mela, apple
melodia, melody
melone (*m.*), melon
membro (*pl.* **membra**), limb
meno, less, minus
menta, mint
mento, chin
mentre, while
meraviglia, marvel
meraviglioso, marvellous, wonderful
mercato, market
mercoledì (*m.*), Wednesday
meridionale, southern
merluzzo, cod, codfish
mese (*m.*), month
messa, Mass
mesto, sad
metà, half (*measure*)
metallo, metal
mettere, to place, put
mezzanotte (*f.*), midnight
mezzo, half
mezzogiorno, midday
mi, me, to me, myself
Michele, Michael
miglio (*pl.* **miglia**) (*f.*), mile
migliore, better
Milano, Milan
milione, million
mille (*pl.* **mila**), thousand
minerale (*m.*), mineral
minuto, minute
mio, my, mine
miracolo, miracle
misterioso, mysterious
mite, mild
mobile (*adj.*), mobile, movable
mobile (*m.*), piece of furniture
moderno, modern
modo, way, manner
moglie (*f.*), wife
molo, pier, quay
molto, much
mondo, world
montagna, monte (*m.*), mountain
morire (*irr.*), to die

mos*a*ico, mosaic
mosca (*pl.* **mosche**), fly
mostra, exhibition
mostrare, to show
mucca (*pl.* **mucche**), cow
mulo, mule
munic*i*pio, Town Hall
muro (*f. pl.* **mura**), wall (*of a city*)
museo, museum
musicale, musical

N

n*a*ilon (*m.*), nylon
N*a*poli, Naples
narrare, to narrate
narrazione (*f.*), story, tale
n*a*scere (*irr.*), to be born
naso, nose
Natale (*m.*), Christmas
naturale, natural
nave (*f.*), ship
ne (*pron.*), of him, of it
ne (*partitive*), some, any
n*e*bbia, fog
negozio (*pl.* **negozi**), shop
nemico, enemy
nero, black
neve (*f.*), snow
nevicare, to snow
Niccolò, Nicholas
niente, nothing
nipote (*m.* or *f.*), nephew, neice
no, no, not
noce (*f.*), nut, walnut
noce di cocco, coconut
noi, we, us
nome (*m.*), name
non, not
nonno, grandfather
nono, ninth
nord (*m.*), north
nostro, our
notare, to note
notte (*f.*), night
novanta, ninety
novantuno, ninety-one
nove, nine
novembre, November
nulla, nothing
n*u*mero, number
numeroso, numerous
nuotare, to swim
nuovo, new
n*u*vola, cloud

O

o, or; **o . . . o,** either . . . or
obbligato, obliged
oca (*pl.* **oche**), goose
occasione (*f.*), occasion
occhiali (*m. pl.*), spectacles
***o*cchio** (*pl.* **occhi**), eye
occidentale, western
occidente (*m.*), west
occupato, busy, occupied
odorare, to smell
odore (*m.*), smell, scent
offrire (*irr.*), to offer
oggetto, object
oggi, today
ogni, every
ogni tanto, now and again
ognuno, everyone, each one
oleandro, oleander
***o*lio,** oil
olivo, olive
ombra, shade
ombrellone (*m.*), large umbrella
onda, wave
onesto, honest
***o*pera,** work, opera
oper*a*io, workman
ora, hour, time
oramai, now, by this time
or*a*rio, timetable
orchestra, orchestra
ordinale, ordinal
ordinare, to order
or*e*cchio, ear
or*e*fice (*m.*), goldsmith
orientale, eastern
oriente (*m.*), East
originale, original
oro, gold
orologio, watch, clock
osare, to dare

osservare, to observe
osso, bone
ottanto, eighty
ottantuno, eighty-one
ottavo, eight
ottenere, to obtain
ottimo, very good
otto, eight
ottobre, October
ottone (*m.*), brass
ovest (*m.*), west
ozioso, idle, lazy

P

pacco, parcel
Padova, Padua
padre, father
paesaggio, landscape
pagare, to pay
pagina, page
paglia, straw
paio (*f. pl.* **paia**), pair
palazzo, palace, mansion
palma, palm (*hand, branch of tree*)
pane (*m.*), bread
panettiere (*m.*), baker
panino, bread roll
panna, cream
panteon (*m.*), Pantheon, temple
Paolo, Paul
papavero, poppy
pappagallo, parrot
paradiso, paradise
parco, park
parecchio, some, considerable (*time*)
parecchi (*pl.*), several, many
parente (*m.* or *f.*), relative
Parigi, Paris
parlare, to speak
parmigiano, Parmesan
parola, word
parte (*f.*), part
partenza, departure
particolarmente, particularly
partire, to leave
Pasqua, Easter
passaporto, passport
passare, to pass; to spend (*time*)
passato, past
passeggiare, to stroll
passeggiata, walk
passeggiero, passenger
pasta, paste (*dough*)
patata, potato
paura, fear
pavimento, floor, pavement
paziente (*adj.*), patient
peggio, worse
pelle (*f.*), skin, leather
pena, sorrow, suffering
pendente, leaning
penisola, peninsula
penna, pen
pensare, to think
pensiero, thought
pepe (*m.*), pepper
per, for, through, by
pera, pear
perchè, why
perciò, therefore
perdere, to lose
perdita, loss
perfetto, perfect
perfino, even
permesso, permission
permesso! allow me! excuse me!
permettere, to allow, to permit
però, however
persona, person
personale, personal
pesante, heavy
pesca (*pl.* **pesche**), peach
pesce (*m.*), fish
pescivendolo, fish-hawker
pesco (*pl.* **peschi**), peach tree
pezzo, piece
piacere (*vb.*), to please
piacere (*m.*), pleasure
  per piacere, please
piacevole, pleasant
piangere, to weep, to cry
pianista (*m.* or *f.*), pianist
piano, floor, storey
pianoforte (*m.*), piano
pianta, plant

piattino, saucer
piatto, plate, dish
piazza, square
p*i*ccolo, small, little
piede (*m.*), foot
pieno, full
pietra, stone
Pietro, Peter
pigliare, to take, catch
pigro, lazy
pineta, pine wood
pioggia, rain
pipa, pipe
pir*a*mide (*f.*), pyramid
pir*o*scafo, steamer
piscina, swimming pool
pisello, pea
pittore (*m.*), painter
pittura, painting
più, more
pl*a*cido, placid
poco, po', little
podere (*m.*), farm
poeta (*m.*), **poetessa** (*f.*), poet
poi, then, afterwards, next
pollo, chicken
polmone (*m.*), lung
polso, wrist
poltrona, armchair
pomer*i*ggio, afternoon
pomodoro, tomato
ponte (*m.*), bridge
porcellana, porcelain, china
porco, pig
porta, door
porta principale, main door
portare, to carry, to bring
porto, harbour, port
porzione (*f.*), portion, share
posizione (*f.*), position
poss*i*bile, possible
posta, post
postino, postman
posto, place
potere (*irr.*), to be able
p*o*vero, poor
pranzare, to dine
pranzo, dinner
pr*a*tico, practical
prato, meadow, lawn
prec*e*dere, to precede
preciso, precise
preferire, to prefer
pregare, to pray
prego! don't mention it!
pr*e*ndere, to catch, to take
preparare, prepararsi, to prepare (*oneself*)
presentare, to present
presente (*adj.*), present
prestare, to lend
presto, soon, quick
prezioso, precious
prezzo, price
primavera, spring
primo, first
princ*i*pale, principal
prob*a*bile, probable
professore (*m.*), **professoressa** (*f.*), professor
profondo, deep, profound
profumo, perfume
programma (*m.*), programme
progresso, progress
pronto, ready: hello (*telephone*)
pronunziare, to pronounce
proprio, own
prosciutto, ham
pr*o*ssimo, next
provare, to prove
prov*i*ncia, province
p*u*bblico, public
pulcino, chick
pulire, to clean
p*u*lpito, pulpit
pure, also, too
puro, pure

Q

quaderno, exercise book
quadrato, square
quadro, picture
qualche, some, any
quale, which, what
quanto? how much?
quaranta, forty

quarantuno, forty-one
quartiere (*m.*), district
quarto, fourth
quasi, almost
quattordici, fourteen
quattro, four
quello, that
quercia, oak, oak-tree
questo, this
qui, here
quindici, fifteen
quinto, fifth

R

raccontare, to relate
radio (*f.*), radio, wireless
ragazzo, -a, boy, girl
raggiungere, to reach
ragione (*f.*), reason
rallentare, to slow down
rapido, fast
rappresentare, to represent
raro, rare
re (*m.*), king
recente, recent
regalo, present, gift
regina, queen
regione (*f.*), region
remare, to row
resistere, to resist
respirare, to breathe
restare, to remain
rete (*f.*), net; luggage rack
ricchezza, wealth
ricco, rich
ricevere, to receive
riconoscere, to recognise
ricordo, souvenir
ridere (*irr.*), to laugh
ridicolo, ridiculous
rifiutare, to refuse
ringraziare, to thank
ripetere, to repeat
riservare, to reserve
riso (*pl.*, **risi**—*m.*), rice
riso (*pl.*, **risa**—*f.*), laughter
risotto, rice dish
rispondere, to answer, reply
risposta, answer
ristorante (*m.*), restaurant
riunire, to assemble
riva, shore
rivedere, to see again
La Riviera, Riviera
Riviera di Levante, eastern Riviera
Riviera di Ponente, western Riviera
rivista, magazine
Roma, Rome
romanesco, Roman style
romano, Roman
romanzo, novel
rosa, rose
rosso, red
rotondo, round
rumore (*m.*), noise

S

sabato, Saturday
sabbia, sand
sala, room
sala d'aspetto, waiting-room
sala da pranzo, dining-room
sale (*m.*), salt
salire, to ascend
salita, ascent
salotto, drawing-room, lounge
salsa, sauce
saltare, to leap, jump
salute (*f.*), health
salvare, to rescue, save
sangue (*m.*), blood
sano, sound, healthy
santo, saint, holy
sapere, to know (*a fact*)
sapone (*m.*), soap
sapore (*m.*), taste
Sardegna, Sardinia
sbaglio, mistake
sbarcare, to land
scala, stair
scarpa, shoe
scatola, box
scegliere (*irr.*), to choose, select
scena, scene, stage
scendere, to descend
sciampagna, champagne

sciarpa, scarf
scivolare, to glide
scompartimento, compartment (*railway*)
scrittore (*m.*), writer
scrivere, to write
scultore (*f.* **-trice**), sculptor, sculptress
scuola, school
scuro, dark
scusare, to excuse
 mi scusi, excuse me
se, if
sè, himself, herself, itself
secolo, century
secondo, second
sedere, sedersi, to sit
sedia, chair
sedia a sdraio, deckchair
sedici, sixteen
segno, sign, mark
seguire, to follow
sei, six
sembrare, to seem, appear
semplice, simple
sempre, always
sentiero, footpath
sentimento, sentiment
senza, without
separare, to separate
sera, evening
 buona sera, good evening
servire, to serve
sessanta, sixty
sessantuno, sixty-one
sesto, sixth
seta, silk
settanta, seventy
settantuno, seventy-one
sette, seven
settembre (*m.*), September
settentrionale, northern
settentrione (*m.*), north
settimana, week
settimo, seventh
sguardo, glance
si, oneself, itself
sì, yes
Sicilia, Sicily
sicuro, safe, certain
sigaretta, cigarette
signor, Mr.
signora, madam, Mrs.; lady
signore, sir; gentleman
signorina, Miss
silenzio, silence
sinistro, left
 a sinistra, to the left
situato, situated
soffiare, to blow
sogliola, sole (*fish*)
sogno, dream
sole (*m.*), sun
solito, usual
soltanto, only
somaro, donkey
sonno, sleep
sopra, on, upon
sorbire, to sip
sorella, sister
sorellina, little sister
sorpresa, surprise
sotto, under
sottopassaggio, subway
Spagna, Spain
Spagnolo, Spanish
spago, string
spalla, shoulder
spandere, to spread out
specchio, mirror
specialmente, especially
spendere, to spend
spesso, thick, frequent
spettacolo, show
spiaggia, beach
spillo, pin
spinaci (*m. pl.*), spinach
splendere, to shine
sportello, door (*carriage or taxi door*)
stagione (*f.*), season
stanco, tired
stanza, room
stanza da bagno, bathroom
stare (*irr.*), to stay, be
stato (*noun*), state
stato (*p.p.* **stare**), been

statua, statue
stazione (*f.*), station
Stefano, Stephen
stella, star
stesso, same
stile (*m.*), style
stirare, to press; to iron
strada, road
strega, witch
stretto, narrow
studente, studentessa, student
studiare, to study
su, on
sud, south
sugo, juice, gravy
suo, his, her
suonare, to sound, to play (*instrument*)
superbo, proud, superb
svago, amusement
Svizzera, Switzerland

T

tappa, halting place
tappeto, carpet, rug
tardi, late
tassì (*m.*), taxi
tavola, table
tazza, cup
tè (*m.*), tea
teatro, theatre
tedesco (*pl.* **tedeschi**), German
telefono, telephone
telegramma (*m.*), telegram
televisione (*f.*), television
temere, to fear
temperino, penknife
tempo, time
temporale (*m.*), storm
tenere, to hold, to keep
tenero, tender
terra, land
terzo, third
tesoro, treasure
testa, head
tetto, roof
ti, you
timido, timid
tirare, to draw
tirreno, Tyrrhenian
Torino, Turin
torre (*f.*), tower
Torre Pendente, Leaning Tower (Pisa)
torta, cake
Toscana, Tuscany
toscano, Tuscan
tovaglia, tablecloth
tovagliolo, serviette, napkin
tramonto, sunset
tranquillo, tranquil
traversata, crossing
tre, three
tredici, thirteen
treno, train
trenta, thirty
trentuno, thirty-one
triglia, mullet
triste, sad
troppo, too, too much
trovare, to find
trovatore, inventor, finder
tu, thou, you
tuffo, plunge, dive
tuo, thy, your
turista (*m.* or *f.*), tourist
tutto, all

U

ucello, bird
udire, to hear
udito, hearing
ufficio, office
ultimamente, lately
ultimo, last
umano, human
umore (*m.*), humour
undicesimo, eleventh
undici, eleven
università (*f.*), university
uno, one
uomo (*pl.* **uomini**), man
uovo (*pl.* **uova**), egg
usanza, custom, usage
uscita, exit
utile, useful
uva, grape, grapes

V

vacanza, vacation
vacca (*pl.* **vacche**), cow
vagone ristorante, dining car (*railway*)
valido, valid
valigia, suitcase
valle (*f.*), valley
vaporetto, steamer
varietà, variety
vario, various
vaso, vase
vecchio, old
vedere (*irr.*), to see
veduta, view, vista
vela, sail
velocità (*f.*), speed
vendere, to sell
venerdì (*m.*), Friday
Venezia, Venice
ventesimo, twentieth
venti, twenty
ventitreesimo, twenty-third
vento, wind
ventuno, twenty-one
veramente, really
verde, green
verità (*f.*), truth
vero, true
versare, to pour
verso, toward
vestibolo, hall, vestibule
vestire, to dress
vetrina, shop window
vetro, glass
vettura, carriage
vi, there; (*pers. pron.*) you, to you
via, street, road
viaggiare, to travel
viaggiatore (*m.*), passenger, traveller
viaggio, journey
viale (*m.*), avenue
vicino, near
vietato, forbidden
vigna, vineyard
villa, country house, villa
villaggio, village
vincere, to win, overcome
vino, wine
violetta, violet
violinista (*m.* or *f.*), violinist
violino, violin
virtù (*f.*), virtue
visibile, visible
visita, visit
visitare, to visit
viso, face
vista, view, sight
vivace, lively
vivere, to live
vivo, alive, lively
voce (*f.*), voice
voglia, desire, longing
voi, you
volere, to want
volta, time, turn
  una volta, once
  due volte, twice
voltare, to turn
volume (*m.*), volume
vostro, your, yours
vuoto, empty

Z

zanzara, mosquito
zero, zero
zia, aunt
zio, uncle
zitto, silent
zoccolo, wooden shoe, clog
zucchero, sugar
zucchino, vegetable marrow

ENGLISH-ITALIAN VOCABULARY

A

about, circa
address, indirizzo
admire, ammirare
Adriatic, Adri*a*tico
aeroplane, aeroplano
after, dopo
afternoon, pomer*i*ggio
afterwards, poi
again, di nuovo, ancora
age, età
agitated, agitato
air, *a*ria
allow, perm*e*ttere
almost, quasi, circa
alphabet, alfabeto
Alps, Alpi (*f. pl.*)
already, già
also, anche, pure
always, sempre
amuse, divertire
amusement, svago, divertimento
ancient, antico
and, e, ed
Andrew, Andrea
anglican, anglicano
animal, animale (*m.*)
ankle, cav*i*glia
Ann, Anna
answer, rispondere (*vb.*); risposta (*noun*)
Anthony, Ant*o*nio
anxious, ansioso
any, alcuno, qualche
appear, sembrare
appetite, appetito
apple, mela
apply, applicare
apricot, albicocca
April, aprile (*m.*)
arcade, galleria
arm, br*a*ccio (*f. pl.* braccia)
armchair, poltrona
around, intorno
arrival, arrivo
arrive, arrivare
art, arte (*f.*)
article, art*i*colo
as, così
ascend, salire
ascent, salita
ash, c*e*nere (*f.*)
ask, domandare, chi*e*dere
assemble, riunire
at, a, ad
attentively, attentamente
audacity, aud*a*cia
August, agosto
aunt, zia
Austria, *A*ustria
automobile, autom*o*bile (*f.*)
autumn, autunno
avenue, viale (*m.*)
avoid, evitare

B

baby, bambino
bad, cattivo
badly, male
baker, panettiere, forn*a*io
balcony, balcone (*m.*)
banana, banana
bank, banca
baptistry, battistero
bar, bar (*m.*)
basilica, bas*i*lica
basket, cestino
bath, bagno
bathroom, stanza da bagno
be, *e*ssere
be able, potere
beach, spi*a*ggia
beautiful, bello
become, diventare

bed, letto
bedroom, *ca*mera
beef, manzo
beefsteak, bistecca
beer, birra
behind, dietro
Belgium, B*e*lgio
believe, cr*e*dere
bell, campana
bell tower, campanile (*m.*)
Berlin, Berlino (*f.*)
better, migliore (*adj.*); m*e*glio (*adv.*)
between, fra, tra
bicycle, bicicletta
big, grande
bill, conto
bird, uccello
birthday, compleanno
biscuit, biscotto
bitter, amaro
black, nero
blond, biondo
blood, sangue (*m.*)
blow (*vb.*), soffiare
blue, azzurro
blue (*pale*), celeste
boat, barca
boiled, boiled meat, lesso
bone, osso
book, libro
both, tutti e due
bottle, bott*i*glia
box, sc*a*tola
boy, ragazzo
brass, ottone (*m.*)
bread, pane (*m.*)
bread-roll, panino
bracelet, braccialetto
breakfast, prima colazione
breathe, respirare
brick, mattone (*m.*)
bridge, ponte (*m.*)
Bridge of Sighs, Ponte dei Sospiri
brief, breve
bring, portare
broth, brodo
brother, fratello
brother-in-law, cognato
brown, bruno
build, edificare, costruire
building, edif*i*cio, edif*i*zio
busy, occupato
but, ma
butcher, macell*a*io
butcher's shop, macelleria
butter, burro
butterfly, farfalla
buy, comprare
by, da, per
Byzantine, bizantino

C

cabbage, c*a*volo
cabin, cabina
cake, torta
calendar, calend*a*rio
calf, vitello
call, chiamare
calm, calmo
camera, m*a*cchina fotogr*a*fica
canal, canale (*m.*)
capital, capitale (*f.*)
cardinal, cardinale
carnation, gar*o*fano
carpet, tappeto
carriage, carrozza
carry, portare
castle, castello
cat, gatto
catch, pr*e*ndere, pigliare
Cathedral, Cattedrale (*f.*), Duomo
Catherine, Caterina
catholic, catt*o*lico
cause, c*a*usa
celebrate, celebrare
celebration, celebrazione (*f.*)
central, centrale
century, s*e*colo
certain, certo
chair, s*e*dia
chalk, gesso
chambermaid, cameriera
champagne, sciampagna
change, cambiare (*vb.*); cambio (*noun*)
Channel (English), M*a*nica

chapel, cappella
chapter, cap*i*tolo
Charles, Carlo
charming, incant*e*vole
chauffeur, autista (*m.* and *f.*)
cheek, gu*a*ncia
cheese, form*a*ggio
chemist, farmacista (*m.* and *f.*)
chemist's shop, farmacia
cheque, assegno
cherry, cili*e*gia
chestnut, castagna, marrone (*m.*)
chew, masticare
chick, pulcino
chicken, pollo
child, bambino, fanciullo
chin, mento
china, porcellana
chocolate, cioccolata
choose, sc*e*gliere
Christmas, Natale (*m.*)
church, chiesa
cigarette, sigaretta
cinema, c*i*nema (*m.*), cinemat*o*grafo
class, classroom, classe (*f.*)
clean, pulire
clearly, chiaramente
climate, clima (*m.*)
clog (*wooden shoe*), zoccolo
close, chi*u*dere (*vb*); vicino (*adv.*)
closed, chiuso
clothes, *a*biti, vestiti (*m. pl.*)
cloud, n*u*vola
coach, vagone (*m.*), carrozza
coast, costa
coat, *a*bito, giacca
cock, gallo
coconut, noce (*f.*) di cocco
cod, merluzzo
coffee, caffè (*m.*)
cold, freddo (*adj.*); raffreddore (*m.*)
collar, colletto
Colosseum, Colosseo
colour, colore (*m.*)
column, colonna
comfortable, c*o*modo
commence, cominciare
communication, comunicazione (*f.*)
compartment, scompartimento
complete, completare
consist, cons*i*stere
continent, continente (*m.*)
continually, continuamente
converse, conversare
cook (*vb.*), cucinare
cooked, cotto
cool, fresco
corner, *a*ngolo
cost, costare
costume, costume (*m.*)
cotton, cotone (*m.*)
country, campagna
court, corte (*f.*), cortile (*m.*)
cousin, cugino
cover, coprire
cow, mucca, vacca
cream, panna, crema
cross, croce (*f.*); attraversare (*vb.*)
crossing, traversata
cry, lacrimare, pi*a*ngere
cup, tazza
cupboard, arm*a*dio
curiosity, curiosità (*f.*)
custom, usanza
customs, dogana
customs officer, doganiere (*m.*)

D

daddy, babbo
dairy, latteria
daisy, margheritina
dance, ballare
dare, osare
daring, aud*a*cia
dark, scuro
daughter, f*i*glia
daughter-in-law, nuora
day, giorno
dear, caro
December, dicembre (*m.*)
decide, dec*i*dere
deck, ponte (*m.*), coperta
deckchair, s*e*dia a sdr*a*io
deep, profondo
definite, definito

delicious, delightful, delizioso, incant*e*vole
departure, partenza
descend, sc*e*ndere
desk, banco, scrivania
dictate, dettare
dictation, dettato
dictionary, dizion*a*rio
die, morire
different, differente
difficult, diff*i*cile
dine, pranzare
dining car, vagone ristorante (*m.*)
dining-room, sala da pranzo
dinner, pranzo
direction, direzione (*f.*)
disappointed, deluso
distance, distanza
distant, lontano, distante
district, quartiere (*m.*)
disturb, disturbare
disturbance, disturbo
divide, div*i*dere
do, fare; see also p. 44, Note
doctor, m*e*dico
dog, cane (*m.*)
doll, b*a*mbola
dome, c*u*pola
donkey, ciuco, *a*sino, somaro
door, porta
door (*carriage*), sportello
draw, tirare
dream, sogno
dress, vestire (*vb.*); *a*bito, veste (*f.*) (*noun*)
drink, bere (b*e*vere) (*vb.*); b*i*bita, bevanda (*noun*)
dry, *a*rido, secco
duck, *a*nitra
dumpling, gnocco

E

each, ciascuno
each one, ognuno
ear, or*e*cchio
early, di buon'ora
east, est, oriente (*m.*)
Easter, Pasqua
eastern, orientale
eastern Riviera, Riviera di Levante
easy, f*a*cile
eat, mangiare
egg, uovo
eight, otto
eighteen, diciotto
eighth, ottavo
eighty, ottanta
either, o
either . . . or, o . . . o
elbow, g*o*mito
electric, el*e*ttrico
elegant, elegante
eleven, *u*ndici
eleventh, undic*e*simo
Elizabeth, Elisabetta
empty, vuotare (*vb.*); vuoto (*adj.*)
enchanting, incant*e*vole
end, fine (*f.*)
enemy, nemico
England, Inghilterra
English, Inglese (*m.* and *f.*); inglese (*adj.*)
enjoy, godere
enter, entrare
entrance, entrata, ingresso
entrance hall, *a*trio
envelope, busta
Epiphany, Epifania
era, *e*poca, era
erase, cancellare
especially, specialmente
etcetera, eccetera (ecc.)
eternal, eterno
Europe, Europa
even, perfino
evening, sera
every, ogni
everyone, ognuno
everywhere, dappertutto
exaggerate, esagerare
example, es*e*mpio
excited, eccitato
excursion, gita, escursione (*f.*)
excuse, scusare
exercise book, quaderno
exhibition, mostra

exit, uscita
exterior, esterno
eye, *o*cchio
eyelash, c*i*glio

F

façade, facciata
face, f*a*ccia, viso
factory, f*a*bbrica
fall, cadere
family, fam*i*glia
fantastic, fant*a*stico
far, lontano
farm, podere (*m.*)
fast, r*a*pido
father, padre
favour, favore (*m.*)
fear, temere (*vb.*); paura (*noun*)
feast, festa
February, febbr*a*io
fertile, f*e*rtile
field, campo
fifteen, qu*i*ndici
fifth, quinto
fifty, cinquanta
final, finale
find, trovare, trovarsi
finger, dito (*f. pl.* dita)
finish, finire
fire, fuoco
first, primo
fish, pesce (*m.*)
fishmonger, pesciv*e*ndolo
five, cinque
flask, fiasco, fiaschetto
floor, piano, pavimento
Florence, Firenze (*f.*)
flower, fiore (*m.*)
fly, mosca
fog, n*e*bbia
follow, seguire
food, cibo
foot, piede (*m.*)
footpath, sentiero
for, per
forbidden, vietato, interdetto
forehead, fronte (*f.*)
foreigner, forestiero, straniero
forest, bosco, foresta
forget, dimenticare
fork, forchetta
forty, quaranta
forum, foro
fountain, fontana
four, quattro
fourteen, quatt*o*rdici
fourth, quarto
France, Fr*a*ncia
Francis, Francesco
free, l*i*bero
French, Francese (*noun*)
French bean, fagiolino
frequent, spesso
fresh, fresco
Friday, venerdì (*m.*)
fried, fritto
friend, amico
from, da
fruit, frutta
fruiterer, fruttiv*e*ndolo
fruit salad, maced*o*nia di frutta
full, pieno
future, futuro, avvenire (*m.*)

G

gallery, galleria
garden, giardino
gay, g*a*io
general, generale
generosity, generosità (*m.*)
Genoa, G*e*nova
gentle, gentile
George, Ge*o*rgio
Germany, Germ*a*nia
German, Tedesco (*noun*)
girl, ragazza
give, dare
glad, contento
glance, sguardo
glass, vetro
glass (*drinking*), bicchiere (*m.*)
glide, scivolare
glove, guanto
go, andare
gold, oro
goldsmith, or*e*fice (*m.*)

gondola, g*o*ndola
gondolier, gondoliere (*m.*)
good, buono
good! splendid! bravo!
goodbye, arrivederci; ciao (*colloq.*)
goose, oca
Gothic, g*o*tica
grammar, gramm*a*tica
Grand Canal, Canal Grande (*m.*)
grandfather, nonno
grandmother, nonna
grape, uva
great, grande
green, verde
guard, conduttore (*m.*)
guide, guidare (*vb.*); guida (*f.*) (*noun*)

H

hair, capello
half, mezzo (*adj.*); metà (*f.*) (*noun*)
hall, vest*i*bolo
ham, prosciutto
hand, mano (*f.*)
handkerchief, fazzoletto
harbour, porto
hat, cappello
have, avere
he, egli, lui, esso
head, capo, testa
health, salute (*f.*)
hear, udire
hearing, udito
heart, cuore (*m.*)
heavy, pesante
help, aiutare
hen, gallina
Henry, Enrico
her, lei, la, (*pron.*); suo (sua, sue, suoi) (*adj.*)
here, qui, qua, ci, vi
here is, ecco
herself, sè, essa, stessa, lei stessa
high, alto
hill, collina
him, lo, lui
himself, sè, egli stesso, lui stesso
hire, impegnare
his, suo (sua, suoi, sue)
hold, tenere
holy, santo
honest, onesto
hope, sperare (*vb.*); speranza (*noun*)
horse, cavallo
hot, caldo
hotel, albergo
hour, ora
house, casa
house (*country*), villa
how, come
however, però
how much (many)? quanto (quanti, -e)?
human, umano
humour, umore (*m.*)
hundred, cento
hungry, to be, aver fame, appetito
husband, marito

I

I, io
ice, ghi*a*ccio
ice-cream, gelato
idea, idea
idle, ozioso
if, se
illuminated, illuminato
imitate, imitare
immense, immenso
important, importante
impression, impressione (*m.*)
in, in
incite, incitare
incitement, incitamento
indeed, infatti
industry, ind*u*stria
inform, informare
information, informazione (*f.*)
inhabitant, abitante (*m.* and *f.*)
ink, inchiostro
inside, dentro
inspection, controllo
inspector, controllore (*m.*)
install, installare
interesting, interessante
interior, interno
invite, invitare

iron, stirare
is, è
island, *i*sola
it, esso, essa, lo, la
  of it, ne
Italian, Italiano (*noun*); italiano (*adj.*)
Italy, It*a*lia
itinerary, itiner*a*rio
itself, si, sè, stesso (a)

J

jacket, giacca
jam, marmellata
James, Gi*a*como
January, genn*a*io
jeweller, gioielliere (*m.*)
jockey, fantino
John, Giovanni
Joseph, Giuseppe
journey, vi*a*ggio
joy, gi*o*ia
Jugoslavia, Iugosl*a*via
juice, sugo
July, l*u*glio
jump, saltare
June, giugno
just, giusto

K

keep, conservare, tenere
key, chiave (*f.*)
kind, gentile
king, re (*m.*)
kiss, baciare (*vb.*); b*a*cio (*noun*)
kitchen, cucina
knee, gin*o*cchio
knife, coltello
know (*fact*), sapere
know (*acquaintance*), con*o*scere

L

lake, lago
lamb, agnello
lamp, l*a*mpada
land, sbarcare (*vb.*); terra (*noun*)
landscape, paes*a*ggio
language, l*i*ngua
large, grande
last, durare (*vb.*); *u*ltimo (*adj.*)
late, tardi
lately, ultimamente
laugh, r*i*dere
lazy, ozioso, pigro
leaf, f*o*glia
leaning, pendente
leap, saltare
learn, imparare
leather, pelle (*f.*), cu*o*io
leave, lasciare, partire
left, sinistro (*adj.*)
leg, gamba
lemon, limone (*m.*)
lemonade, limonata
lemon squash, (una) spremuta di limone
lend, prestare
less, meno
lesson, lezione (*f.*)
let, affittare, lasciare
letter, l*e*ttera
library, biblioteca
life, vita
lift, ascensore (*m.*)
light, luce (*f.*), lume (*m.*) (*noun*); leggero (*adj.*)
lily, g*i*glio
limb, membro (*f. pl.* membra)
limpid, l*i*mpido
lip, labbro (*pl.* labbra)
liquor, liquore (*m.*)
listen, ascoltare
literature, letteratura
little, p*i*ccolo (*adj.*); poco (*adv.*)
live (*dwell*), abitare
local, locale
London, Londra
long, lungo
long (*for*), bramare
look (*at*), guardare
look (*for*), cercare
lose, p*e*rdere
loss, p*e*rdita
Louis, Luigi
lounge, salotto
love, amare (*vb.*); amore (*m.*) (*noun*)

low, basso
luggage, bag*a*glio
luggage rack, rete (*f.*)
lunch, colazione (*f.*)
lung, polmone (*m.*)

M

machine, m*a*cchina
Madam (Mrs.), signora
magazine, rivista
magnificent, magn*i*fico
major, maggiore
make, fare
Mamma, mamma
man, uomo
manner, modo
mansion, palazzo
map, carta geogr*a*fica
marble, marmo
March, marzo
Margaret, Margherita
Marius, M*a*rio
mark (*sign*), segno
Mark, Marco
market, mercato
marmalade, marmellata
marrow (*vegetable*), zucchino
Martin, Martino
marvel, meravi*g*lia
Mary, Maria
mass, messa
master, maestro
masterpiece, capolavoro
match, cerino
May, m*a*ggio
me, mi, me
meadow, prato
meantime, meanwhile, intanto
meat, carne (*f.*)
medicine, medicina
medieval, medioevale
Mediterranean, Mediterr*a*neo
meet, incontrare
melody, melodia
melon, melone (*m.*)
metal, metallo
Michael, Michele
midday, mezzogiorno
middle, m*e*dio
midnight, mezzanotte (*f.*)
Milan, Milano (*f.*)
mild, mite
mile, m*i*glio
milk, latte (*m.*)
million, milione (*m.*)
mine, mio (mia, miei, mie)
mint, menta
minute, minuto
miracle, mir*a*colo
mirror, sp*e*cchio
Miss, signorina
mistake, sb*a*glio
mobile, m*o*bile
modern, moderno
Monday, lunedì (*m.*)
money, denaro, danaro
month, mese (*m.*)
moon, luna
more, più
morning, mattina
motorboat, motoscafo
mosaic, mos*a*ico
mosquito, zanzara
mother, madre (*f.*)
mountain, montagna, monte (*m.*)
mouth, bocca
Mr., Signor, il signor . . .
much, molto
mule, mulo
mullet, tr*i*glia
museum, museo
musical, musicale
my, mio (mia, miei, mie)
myself, mi, me stesso(-a)
mysterious, misterioso

N

name, nome (*m.*)
namely, cioè
Naples, N*a*poli
narrate, narrare
narrow, stretto
natural, naturale
naughty, cattivo
near, vicino
neck, collo

need, aver bisogno di (*vb.*); bisogno (*noun*)
net, rete (*f.*)
new, nuovo
newsagent, giornal*a*io
newspaper, giornale (*m.*)
next, venturo, pr*o*ssimo (*adj.*); poi (*adv.*)
night, notte (*f.*)
nine, nove
nineteen, diciannove
ninety, novanta
ninth, nono
no, no
noise, rumore (*m.*)
north, nord, settentrione (*m.*)
northern, settentrionale
nose, naso
not, non; **not any,** nessuno (-a)
note, notare
nothing, niente, nulla (*m.*)
novel, romanzo
November, novembre (*m.*)
now, ora, adesso
  by now, oramai
number, n*u*mero
numerous, numeroso
nut, noce (*f.*)
nylon, n*a*ilon (*m.*)

O

oak, qu*e*rcia
object, oggetto
observe, osservare
obtain, ottenere
occasion, occasione (*f.*)
October, ottobre (*m.*)
of, di; see also p. 61
offer, offrire
office, uff*i*cio
oil, *o*lio
old, v*e*cchio
oleander, oleandro
olive, olivo
omelette, frittata
on, sopra, su; see also p. 61
one, uno, una
oneself, si, se stesso, se stessa
onion, cipolla
only, soltanto, solo, solamente, non . . . che; see p. 127
open, aprire
or, o; **either . . . or,** o . . . o
orange, ar*a*ncia
orangeade, aranciata
orchestra, orchestra
order, ordinare
ordinal, ordinale
original, originale
other, altro
otherwise, altrimenti
our, nostro
outside, fuori
own, pr*o*prio
ox, bue
oxen, buoi

P

Padua, P*a*dova
page, p*a*gina
pain, pena, dolore (*m.*)
painter, pittore (*m.*)
painting, pittura
pair, p*a*io
palace, palazzo
palm, palma
panorama, panorama
paper, carta
paradise, paradiso
parcel, pacco
parent, genitore (*m.*)
Paris, Parigi (*f.*)
park, parco
Parmesan, parmigiano
parrot, pappagallo
part, parte (*f.*)
particular, particolare
pass, passare
passage, corrid*o*io
passenger, passeggiero, viaggiatore (*m.*)
passport, passaporto
past, passato, scorso
paste (*dough*), pasta
patient, paziente
Paul, P*a*olo

pavement, pavimento
paw, zampa
pay, pagare
pea, pisello
peach, pesca
pear, pera
peasant, contadino
pen, penna
pencil, matita
peninsula, pen*i*sola
penknife, temperino
people, gente (*f.*)
pepper, pepe (*m.*)
perfect, perfetto
perfume, profumo
perhaps, forse
permission, permesso
permit, perm*e*ttere
person, persona
personal, personale
Peter, Pietro
petrol, benzina
photograph, fotografia
piano, pianoforte (*m.*)
pianist, pianista (*m.* and *f.*)
picture, quadro
piece, pezzo
pier, molo
pig, maiale, porco
pillow, guanciale (*m.*)
pin, spillo
pinewood, pineta
pipe, pipa
place, m*e*ttere (*vb.*); luogo, posto (*noun*)
placid, pl*a*cido
plant, pianta
plate, piatto
platform, marciapiede (*m.*), banchina
play (*games*), giocare
pleasant, piac*e*vole
please, per piacere, per favore
pleased, contento
poet, poeta (*m.*)
poor, p*o*vero
poppy, pap*a*vero
porcelain, porcellana
porter, facchino
portion, porzione (*f.*)
position, posizione (*f.*)
possible, poss*i*bile
post, posta
postcard, cartolina
potato, patata
pour, versare
practical, pr*a*tico
precious, prezioso
precise, preciso
prefer, preferire
prepare, preparare; (*get ready*) prepararsi
present, presentare (*vb.*); presente (*adj.*)
present (*gift*), regalo, dono
press, stirare
price, prezzo
principal, principale
probable, prob*a*bile
proceed, proc*e*dere
professor, professore (*m.*), professoressa (*f.*)
profound, profondo
programme, programma (*m.*)
progress, progresso
pronounce, pronunziare
proud, superbo
prove, provare
proverb, prov*e*rbio
province, prov*i*ncia
public, p*u*bblico
pulpit, p*u*lpito
pupil, alunno (-a)
put, m*e*ttere
pyramid, pir*a*mide (*f.*)

Q

quay, molo
queen, regina
question, domanda
queue, fila, coda
quick, presto
quite, assai

R

rabbit, con*i*glio
race, corsa

radio, r*a*dio (*f.*)
railway, ferrovia
railway-line, bin*a*rio
rain, pi*o*ggia
raise, alzare; (*get up*) alzarsi
rare, raro
raspberry, lampone (*m.*)
raw, crudo
reach, raggi*u*ngere
read, l*e*ggere
ready, pronto
really, veramente
reason, ragione (*f.*)
receive, ric*e*vere
recognise, ricon*o*scere
red, rosso
refuse, rifiutare
region, regione (*f.*)
relate, raccontare
relative, parente (*m.* and *f.*)
remain, restare
repeat, rip*e*tere
reply, risp*o*ndere
represent, rappresentare
rescue, salvare
reserve, riservare
resist, res*i*stere
rest, riposare
restaurant, ristorante (*m.*)
retain, conservare
Rialto Bridge (Venice), Ponte di Rialto
rice, riso
rich, ricco
right, destro
ring, suonare (*vb.*); anello (*noun*)
river, fiume (*m.*)
road, via, strada
roast, arrosto
Robert, Roberto
Roman, romano
Rome, Roma
roof, tetto
room, sala, stanza
rose, rosa
round, rotondo
row, remare (*vb.*); fila (*noun*)
rug, tappeto

S

sad, mesto, triste
safe, sicuro
sail, vela
saint, santo
salad, insalata
salt, sale (*m.*)
same, stesso
sand, s*a*bbia
Sardinia, Sardegna
satisfied, contento
Saturday, s*a*bato
sauce, salsa
saucer, piattino
save, salvare
say, dire
scarf, sciarpa
scene, scena
school, scuola
sculptor, scultore (*m.*)
sea, mare (*m.*)
seashore, marina
season, condire (*vb.*); stagione (*f.*, *noun*)
second, secondo
see, vedere
seem, sembrare
select, sc*e*gliere
sell, v*e*ndere
send, mandare
sentence, frase (*f.*)
sentiment, sentimento
separate, separare
September, settembre (*m.*)
servant, dom*e*stico
serve, servire
serviette, tovagliolo
seven, sette
seventeen, diciassette
seventh, s*e*ttimo
seventy, settanta
several, parecchi, par*e*cchie
shade, ombra
she, ella, essa, lei
sheet, lenzuolo
sheet of paper, f*o*glio
shine, spl*e*ndere, brillare
ship, nave (*f.*)

shoe, scarpa
shop, negozio, bottega
shore, riva
short, corto, breve
shoulder, spalla
shout, gridare
show, mostrare (*vb.*): spettacolo (*noun*)
Sicily, Sicilia
sick, ammalato, malato
sideboard, credenza
sigh, sospiro
sign, segno
silence, silenzio
silk, seta
silver, argento
simple, semplice
sing, cantare
sip, sorbire
sister, sorella
sister-in-law, cognata
sit, sedere, sedersi
situated, situato
six, sei
sixteen, sedici
sixth, sesto
sixty, sessanta
skin, pelle (*f.*)
sky, cielo
sleep, dormire (*vb.*); sonno (*noun*)
slow, lento
slow down, rallentare
small, piccolo
smell, odorare (*vb.*); odore (*noun*)
smoke, fumare
snow, nevicare (*vb.*); neve (*f.*, *noun*)
so, così
soap, sapone (*m.*)
sole (*fish*), sogliola
some, alcuno (-a, -i, -e); qualche
son, figlio
son-in-law, genero
soon, presto
sound, suonare, sonare (*vb.*); suono (*noun*)
south, sud, mezzogiorno
southern, meridionale
souvenir, ricordo
Spain, Spagna
Spanish, spagnolo
speak, parlare
spectacles, occhiali
speed, velocità (*f.*)
spend, spendere (*money*); passare (*time*)
spinach, spinaci (*m. pl.*)
spire, guglia
splendid! bravo!
spoon, cucchiaio
spring, primavera
square (*geometrical*), quadrato
square, piazza
stage, scena
stair, scala
stamp, francobollo
star, stella
state, stato
station, stazione (*f.*)
station master, capostazione (*m.*)
statue, statua
stay, stare (*vb.*); soggiorno (*noun*)
steamer, vaporetto, piroscafo
Stephen, Stefano
still, ancora
stocking, calza
stone, pietra
stop, fermare, fermarsi (*vb.*); fermata (*noun*)
storey, piano
storm, temporale (*m.*)
story, narrazione (*f.*), racconto
straw, paglia
strawberry, fragola
street, via
string, spago
strong, forte
student, studente (*m.*), studentessa (*f.*)
study, studiare (*vb.*); studio (*noun*)
style, stile, moda (*dress*)
subway, sottopassaggio
sugar, zucchero
suitcase, valigia
summer, estate (*f.*, *noun*); estivo (*adj.*)
sun, sole

sunburnt, abbronzato
Sunday, dom*e*nica
sunset, tramonto
supper, cena
sure, certo
surprise, sorpresa
sweet, dolce
swim, nuotare (*vb.*); nuotata (*noun*)
swimming pool, piscina
swimsuit, costume de bagno
Switzerland Sv*i*zzera

T

table, t*a*vola
tablecloth, tov*a*glia
tail, coda
take, pr*e*ndere, pigliare
tale, narrazione (*f.*), novella
tall, alto
tanned, abbronzato
taste, sapore (*m.*), gusto
taxi, tassì (*m.*)
tea, tè (*m.*)
teach, insegnare
tear, l*a*crima
teaspoon, cucchiaino
telegram, telegramma (*m.*)
telephone, tel*e*fono
television, televisione (*f.*)
ten, dieci
tender, t*e*nero
tenth, d*e*cimo
thank, ringraziare
thanks, ringraziamenti (*m. pl.*)
that, che, ciò, quello
that is to say, cioè
the, l', il, la, lo, i, le, gli
theatre, teatro
themselves, si, sè, se stessi, se stesse
then, allora, poi, dunque
there, là, lì, vi
therefore, dunque, perciò
they, loro, essi (-e)
thick, spesso, denso
thief, ladro
thing, cosa
think, pensare
third, terzo
thirteen, tr*e*dici
thirty, trenta
this, questo (*adj.*); ciò (*pron.*)
thou, tu
thought, pensiero
thousand, mille (*m.*) (*pl.* mila)
thread, filo
three, tre
throat, gola
through, per, attraverso
throw, buttare
Thursday, giovedì (*m.*)
thus, così
thy, tuo (tua, tue, tuoi)
ticket, biglietto
tie, cravatta
time, tempo, volta
timetable, or*a*rio
timid, t*i*mido
tired, stanco
to, a, ad
toast, brindare (*vb.*); br*i*ndisi (*m.*) (*noun*)
today, oggi
toffee, caramella
together, insieme
tomato, pomodoro
tomorrow, domani
tongue, l*i*ngua
too anche
tooth, dente (*m.*)
tour, girare (*vb.*); giro, gita (*noun*)
touring car, torpedone (*m.*)
tourist, turista (*m.* and *f.*)
toward, verso
towel, asciugamano
tower, torre (*f.*)
town, città (*f.*)
town hall, munic*i*pio
train, treno
tranquil, tranquillo
traveller, viaggiatore (*m.*); (*f.* -trice)
treasure, tesoro
tree, *a*lbero
true, vero
truth, verità (*f.*)

Tuesday, martedì (*m.*)
tumbler, bicchiere (*m.*)
tunnel, galleria
Turin, Torino
Tuscan, toscano
Tuscany, Toscana
twelve, d*o*dici
twentieth, vent*e*simo
twenty, venti
two, due
Tyrrhenian, Tirreno

U

ugly, brutto
umbrella (*large*), ombrellone (*m.*)
uncertain, incerto
uncle, zio
under, sotto
understand, capire
ungrateful, ingrato
university, università (*f.*)
upon, sopra
us, ci, noi
useful, *u*tile
usual, s*o*lito
usually, di s*o*lito

V

vacant, l*i*bero
vacation, vacanza
valid, v*a*lido
valley, valle (*f.*)
variety, varietà (*f.*)
various, v*a*rio
vase, vaso
veal, vitello
vegetable, legume (*m.*), verdura
Venice, Ven*e*zia
very, molto, assai
very good, *o*ttimo
vestibule, vest*i*bolo
Victor, Vitt*o*rio
view, veduta, vista
village, vill*a*ggio
vinegar, aceto
vineyard, vigna
violet, violetta
violinist, violinista (*m.* and *f.*)
visible, vis*i*bile
visit, visitare (*vb.*); v*i*sita (*noun*)
vivid, vivo
voice, voce (*f.*)
volume, volume (*m.*)

W

wait, aspettare
waiter, cameriere (*m.*)
waiting room, sala d'aspetto
waitress (*maid*), cameriera
walk, camminare, passeggiare (*vb.*); passeggiata (*noun*)
wall, muro, parete (*f.*)
want, volere, desiderare (*vb.*); bisogno (*noun*)
wardrobe, arm*a*dio
wash, lavare
watch, orol*o*gio
water, acqua
watermelon, coc*o*mero
wave, onda
wax, cera
way, modo
we, noi
weak, d*e*bole
wealth, ricchezza
Wednesday, mercoledì (*m.*)
week, settimana
weep, lacrimare, pi*a*ngere
welcome, gradito (*adj.*); benvenuto (*noun*)
well, pozzo (*noun*); bene (*adv.*); sano (*adj.*)
west, ovest (*m.*); occidente (*m.*); ponente (*m.*)
western, occidentale
western Riviera, Riviera di Ponente
what, that which, che cosa, che, quale, quello che, ciò che
where, dove
which, che, cui, quale?
while, mentre
white, bianco
who, chi? che, cui
whom, chi? che, cui
whose, di chi? a chi?
why, perchè

wide, largo
wife, m*o*glie, sposa
William, Guglielmo
wind, vento
window, finestra
window (*small*), finestrino
wine, vino
winter, inverno
wish, volere (*vb.*); aug*u*rio (*pl.* auguri) (*noun*)
witch, strega
with, con
within, dentro
without, senza
woman, donna
wonderful, meraviglioso
wood (*forest*), bosco, foresta
wood (*firewood*), legno, legna
wool, lana
word, parola
work, lavorare (*vb.*); *o*pera, lavoro (*noun*)
workman, oper*a*io
world, mondo
wrist, polso
write, scr*i*vere
writer, scrittore (*m.*)

Y

year, anno
yearn, bramare
yearning, bramo
yellow, giallo
yes, sì
yesterday, ieri
yet, ancora
you, Lei, Loro, tu, ti, te, vi, voi
young, gi*o*vane
your, Suo, tuo, vostro, Loro
yours truly, vostro (Suo) devot*i*ssimo (*abb.* devmo)
youth, gi*o*vane (*m.*); giovanotto, giovinezza

Z

zero, zero
zone, zona

INDEX